'Business marketing in these times dominated by social media influencers is confusing at best. Until now. *Boost Your Marketing ROI* is a breath of fresh air. This book takes a grassroots approach to establishing a marketing presence in a noisy world, written by someone whose own business journey has seen her move from struggling restaurateur to successful business owner, marketer, trainer and software developer. A highly recommended read.'
— **Jennie Matthews**, Jenanco Business Solutions

'Very simple to read. A common-sense way that literally shows me how to do marketing and why. There were so many things to learn, I felt the author really cared about giving me all the information she had. I also enjoyed the stories at the end of each section, it felt like I was being given one-on-one advice. Overall, an excellent marketing resource.'
— **Dr Tarn McLean**, Ocre Designs

'This book is comprehensive in covering everything you need to know to start marketing your business. It is full of great content and real-world examples. It covers the basics of marketing, business processes, types of marketing – everything you need to know to start marketing your business. An enjoyable read.'
— **Kate Fabian**, AppIT Consulting

'The information in the book is genuine, structured and logical. The methodology is applicable to any business aiming to get positive results. I learned about some of the most critical elements of marketing, from traditional to online. The methodology was structured, easy to understand and logically sequenced. A great piece of work.'
— **Dr Glashie Qudsia**, Simple Profit Solutions

'A book I found useful for my own small business. Straightaway I saw what I could do to get started on my marketing campaigns. I saw it as a great resource for my friends who are also starting businesses. It is easy to read and follow. The real-life examples from the author's own experience helped me to think about ideas I could use for my campaigns and to look at what other yoga teachers do.'
— **Angie Topham**, Levanta Yoga Studio

'There are so many areas covered in this book that it is informative, easy to read and has a lot of depth. I find marketing is the area where people are most prone to losing money in their business, but this book helps the reader break down marketing with real-life business cases empowering the reader with practical support.'
— **Yvette Suss**, AMT Solutions

BOOST YOUR MARKETING ROI

A systematic approach to get better results

Miriam van Heusden

Rethink

First published in Great Britain in 2021
by Rethink Press (www.rethinkpress.com)

This book is dedicated to my son Lachlan,
my inspiration

Contents

Introduction

When you run a business, you are excited and proud to be operating your own enterprise. But marketing your business may be an area where you lack knowledge or skills. It is a huge topic that requires vast expertise.

I know how difficult it can be to find and apply the right marketing strategy for your business. I have owned and operated three restaurants – serving over 2,500 customers per week and turning over close to $1 million annually – and have implemented an extensive marketing mix of different promotional and advertising campaigns. My goal was to attract more customers to the business and for customers to spend more money or visit more often.

The inspiration for this book stems from my work developing a software program that tracks marketing campaign performance. I specifically designed this program for small to medium-size business owners who want to run effective mixed-marketing campaigns including advertising, promotions, loyalty programmes, competitions and such. After my restaurant owner days, I worked as a vocational trainer, achieving qualifications in management, hospitality, business, and marketing. During this time, I had the opportunity to research the development and customer validation for the new software. I was interested to see if other business owners experienced the same issues I had when running my businesses. I wanted to know what their main problems were, as well as their software wants and needs, so I could provide the solution.

The result of this work was Maralytics: a piece of software that tracks and reports on all marketing performance results. It is specifically designed to provide one-step tracking for any type of marketing activity; the dashboard shows all campaign results, making it easy to decide how to spend your precious marketing dollars more effectively. My research told me that, for many, marketing is a daunting and often overwhelming challenge. I knew it was important to have products and services to support business owners with marketing plans covering social media, email marketing, organic content marketing and any other options they might need.

Most business owners hate wasting money. In my research, I found that the most common frustration for business owners is difficulty attracting new customers. Most think marketing requires a lot of work and knowledge and they do not have the time, direction, or inclination to do anything about it. They are too busy concentrating on their businesses, with their immediate demands and priorities. Often, they do a bit of everything in their marketing in the hope that something will work.

When you do not know where to start to create a marketing strategy, and you do not have a tracking system to monitor results or the data to create reports, you make business decisions based on hope, guesswork and crossing your fingers. This makes it difficult to operate other areas in the business, such as creating budgets, forecasting and being proactive in growing the business. You may miss vital information that could make a difference to attracting new customers and retaining existing ones.

The only way a business survives is through customers spending money. Revenue is what keeps a business operating: it pays for the rent, staff, resources and your time. You want to make sure you maximise every dollar you spend to attract customers so you can get the best return on your marketing investment. For your business to succeed, you need a strategy to attract customers to provide a steady flow of sales and revenue.

When you can plan, implement, track, measure and report on all marketing activities, everything becomes easier. You avoid wasting money on ineffective campaigns and focus on the ones that work. You attract more customers and bring in more revenue. You can even forecast so that you have a steady cashflow in the future.

In this book, I go through the Maralytics five-step methodology to provide you with a way to attract more customers and revenue to your business, for less money and effort than you are currently doing.

This five-step methodology includes:

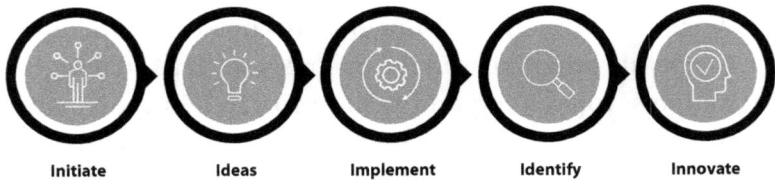

| Initiate | Ideas | Implement | Identify | Innovate |

- **Initiate:** This first step is about planning and preparation. We look at why you need marketing plans, goals and budgets in your business. This is about how you want to grow your business and meet the needs of your customers. Spending time preparing a roadmap for your marketing makes success much easier to achieve. The more you put into this step, the less stress and distraction there will be later. By having a plan and a budget, you will know exactly what you need to do, when you need to do it, and will have the required resources ready. Every successful activity is the result of good planning and implementation.

- **Ideas:** Here we look at all the possibilities for your marketing mix, with ideas and inspiration to help you boost your results in the slow times and accelerate your progress toward your goals. Being active on different channels enhances your visibility, maintains your reputation, wins you new customers and helps your business to stay at the front of your customers' minds. In this section, we look in detail at the components of online, digital and traditional channels to amplify your brand. The opportunities are endless, with new channels appearing regularly. The types of campaigns and activities you can use are unlimited. When your business is more visible, your prospective customers will find you much more easily.

- **Implement:** This section will help you to turn your plans and ideas into real-life actions to increase performance in your business. Taking advantage of sales cycles and trends will accelerate the impact of your current or newly created practices. Implementation is critical for success. It is the beating heart of your marketing plans and the actual 'doing' of the planned activities.

- **Identify:** This section is about getting to know what you want and how you can get it. Breaking everything down into smaller chunks gives a clearer picture on what you want to achieve, the difference you want to make with your business and the results you desire. When you are clear on this, it is much easier to allocate energy and funds efficiently – you can focus your marketing efforts in the most cost-effective way. Drill down further into how to create the key outcomes you are aiming for and find out the impact good decisions can have on your business.

- **Innovate:** The last step in the process is to review what has been done in the past and create the future, using analytics, historical data and optimisation to create your winning formula. Once you have analysed your results, you can look at strategies to improve your marketing efforts and maximise your desired outcomes. When you use forecasting methods to help predict the future, you can find new ways to stand out from the crowd. By being innovative, you can attract more customers with less effort or funds. This allows you to spend more time developing your business rather than responding to day-to-day events.

By following these five steps, you can create a person-alised marketing system that is perfect for your business. This can be done in any industry. You want your business to be able to thrive in any climate and good marketing is the key to attracting customers and revenue.

Creating a personalised marketing system means you will know where to focus your efforts, can generate reports for review and analysis and make decisions that improve the performance of your business. The simpler the system, the easier it is to implement and have your team follow.

If you own a business and do your own marketing, this book is for you. Get better results, be proactive in every aspect of your marketing and increase your business success.

Let's get started.

PART ONE

INITIATE

You will always need to market your business. It is the way you attract your ideal customers and convince them that your product is better than the competition. Marketing is not sales. Sales are the result of good marketing.

Every business is different and requires unique marketing tactics. Some businesses require a lot of marketing while others require very little (eg due to their location, having a niche product or service, or a product or service that is in high demand/a current trend). The process of building a plan, sticking to it and allocating the time and resources needed for it to succeed, is the secret to successful marketing.

Without a plan, there is no direction. Without preparation, there is inconsistency and chaos. Without customers, your business cannot survive.

To attract customers, you need to understand the value of your product or service and how marketing can enhance what you have on offer. People are unlikely to come to your business or buy from you if they do not know the 'who, what, where, when and why' of your product or service. Improved performance is not about discovering a particular growth strategy that is being promoted on the internet or following the latest trend in digital marketing. It is about leveraging the resources you already have and making the most of what they can do for your business' bottom line.

Effective marketing is a key growth driver for every business. A good marketing system creates control, guides priorities, generates processes, gives account-ability and is a way to create and measure profit. Doing the planning, collecting resources, and having all the elements ready are the first steps to initiating a good marketing system and toolkit.

1
Planning

A marketing plan helps you promote your products and services to meet your business goals and customer requirements.[1] This is a document that outlines the activities you will do to attract customers to your business. To create a good marketing plan takes time, research and commitment. The process involves:

- Identifying your target market.

- Understanding how your product or service meets customers' needs.

- Identifying your competitors and their strengths and weaknesses.

---

1   Business.gov.au, 'How to write your marketing plan' (10 March 2021), https://business.gov.au/Planning/Business-plans/How-to-write-your-marketing-plan, accessed 20 May 2021

- Positioning your brand, products and services so that your target market sees your business.

- Setting goals for your marketing activities.

- Establishing a strategy to reach your target market that identifies the channels and tools you will use to do this.

A good marketing plan is like a strategic road map that helps you to plan, implement and track your marketing activities. There are lots of templates for marketing plans available – search on the internet for a version that works for you and your business. A shorter marketing plan will briefly cover the basics. A longer marketing plan goes into different aspects of your business; this type of plan is especially important when you start your business or are in your first year of operation.

Planning benefits

Most business owners I have met do not have a marketing plan. Their main priority is to spend time working in the business and running operations. This is where they thrive and can demonstrate their expertise and gain confidence. Marketing is an area of the business that is either not important to them, they do not know what to do or where to start, or how to create a plan. They see it as a waste of time and not relevant to the daily activities of their businesses.

A marketing plan enables you to attract more customers and make more money. With a plan in place, your business can operate proactively rather than reactively. It gives you a competitive advantage and a systematic approach that enables the business to grow and succeed.

THE MERITS OF A MARKETING PLAN

When I owned my restaurants, I would run competitions for my customers throughout the year. I wanted to make sure that all the quiet times periods of the year had something going on to keep customers engaged and attract new ones at the same time.

It was vital to plan every component; activity planning, negotiating a prize with a resort, having promotional posters and an entry form designed by a graphic designer, printing posters and entry forms, co-ordinating social media blasts, training staff, uploading data entry, notifying the entry winner, and evaluating post-campaign. It took three competitions for me to perfect a good system.

These competitions had to be worked into the yearly marketing plan so I could see what activities were happening during the year, what they entailed and when they were happening to make sure there weren't any activity or resource clashes.

A good marketing plan gives you:

- Better time management
- A consistent structure for marketing activities
- More accurate content
- The power to delegate
- An aligned business where everyone is on the same page
- A vision that is supported by current activities
- A roadmap for the activities that are required for increasing brand awareness and sales
- Clear, achievable and measurable goals
- An executable strategy
- Customer awareness (understanding your customers, who they are and how to attract more of them)
- Competitor awareness (knowing what they are doing and what opportunities they are not utilising that you could be)
- Brand visibility to attract new customers and develop a relationship with your customers
- An accurate budget for your marketing expenses and effective use of your resources

This is not an exhaustive list, and you may discover other benefits once you put your marketing plan into action. There are many resources available to help you create a marketing plan that fits the needs of your business, and it is easy to find support if you need it.

PLANNING YOUR YEAR AHEAD

For my second restaurant, I would create the marketing plan each January. In this plan, I listed every campaign, promotion and competition I was expecting to run that year. I noted when the activity deadlines were, the budgets for advertisements and how/where they would be allocated. This included sponsorship events for Jeans for Genes Day and Royal Society for the Prevention of Cruelty to Animals (RSPCA) Happy Tails Day, such as selling their merchandise, dressing up and matching menu specials to these charities. By planning all of the campaigns and strategies for the year ahead and adding them to my marketing plan and diary, I could be highly effective in creating promotions to increase traffic in the quieter times and regulate cashflow for the business while taking advantage of the busier times by increasing the average customer spend through upselling opportunities.

Action plans

An action plan includes an overview of the activities and steps you want to pursue in the short term.

An action plan can be created for every aspect of marketing, for every strategy, campaign or initiative you carry out. The reason why most businesses create an action plan is to keep the momentum flowing from their main marketing plan.

Action plans are good to use in conjunction with a calendar, so you can balance your activities and consider the different seasons and events that happen throughout the year. By visualising the next year and breaking it down into quarters and months, you can plan when you want your marketing events and activities to take place in order to make progress in your marketing plan and meet the overall goals of your business.

Having ideas for marketing activities in your head is not a plan. You cannot rely on memory. There is no structure, consistency, or way of sharing the information with other people. When it is in your head, you do not have access to the information needed to plan or review activities. It is vital that you document this information, as it can be used as historical data when forecasting. An action plan is also necessary for delegating to your team or outsourcing tasks to contractors.

FAILING TO PLAN MEANS MISSING OUT

The first year I helped organise the school fair, I met the marketing manager at my local Bunnings Warehouse in May to request donation items for October. I was told that it was too late in the year to request items as their fundraising budget for that year had already been allocated. Their marketing action plans were created in January and approved by upper management by the end of February, so I missed out on getting any items for the auction. The next year, I knew the deadline and planned for it.

Marketing goals

Marketing goals distil what the business wants to achieve with its marketing as a component of the business plan. They are used to create and measure the marketing performance element of the business' success. Goals provide a direction and purpose, helping you to focus.

Clear goals are more achievable. They should be written in a way that communicates exactly what you want to accomplish in marketing your business. Having a variety of goals ensures you have a balanced marketing plan capable of achieving your business' vision.

Your marketing goals should align with the business goals, as both are linked to growth, performance and customer acquisition. Marketing goals support the achievement of the overall business vision. The goals are how to fulfil that vision. Goals can be short term, long term or for the length of the business' existence.

Five to six is the optimal amount of marketing goals for a business, providing something to strive toward.

When there are no goals, the business has no direction; eventually, it will lose momentum and operations will suffer.

Some good examples of marketing goals are:

- To build brand awareness
- To generate a high volume of customers or leads
- To improve customer satisfaction
- To increase sales/profit/revenue

These goals are the endpoints that you want to achieve through your marketing. Once you are clear on your goals, you can create objectives, strategies and campaigns to reach them.

SETTING YOUR MARKETING GOALS

The main marketing goals for all my restaurants were to create brand awareness and attract more customers to the venue. To achieve these, I used a good mix of marketing activities that worked well and complemented the restaurants' values while helping me to achieve my business vision.

Marketing budget

Most big businesses allocate a percentage of their revenue to be spent on marketing; many small businesses do not. According to Investopedia,[2] 67% of small businesses fail in the first ten years. The most common reasons for failure are marketing mishaps and poor budgeting, where a small business underestimates its business costs and does not establish realistic budgets for current and future marketing needs.

For most business owners, it is critical to look at where you spend your marketing budget. You must spend money wisely to get a good return on investment (ROI) for your activities. Decide how much money you are willing to allocate to your marketing budget and put this number into your marketing plan as your budgeting spend. Once you have committed to a figure in your budget, you can distribute it between the different activities you have listed in your strategies and campaigns. Your budget and action plan work together. If you do not have a marketing plan and an action plan, you do not have direction. If you do not have a budget, it is easy to waste money and spend it on the wrong things.

Some marketing activities may not cost money, for example content posts on social media. Uploading posts on social media is not in itself a marketing plan or a strategy to attract new customers to your business, but it is a cost-effective way to promote brand awareness to your customers. By consistently posting interesting or informative content, you can keep your

---

2   M Horton, 'The 4 most common reasons a small business fails', Investopedia (31 March 2021), www.investopedia.com/articles/personal-finance/120815/4-most-common-reasons-small-business-fails.asp, accessed 20 May 2021

audience engaged and attract followers to spend money in your business.

While this type of marketing activity does not cost money, it does take time. Time to shoot the photo, to upload the photo and to check the activity on the post. This time has a monetary value, which needs to be priced as a dollar amount. It is the same for blogs or articles. If you spend time researching and writing stories, you need to cost this time and factor it into your budget. Always add up the hours you spend on 'free' marketing activities; an easy way to calculate this is by considering how much you would have to pay someone to do this for you.

You need to calculate your marketing budget within your overall business budget. Depending on your business or industry, this could be anywhere from 3% to 20% of your gross revenue. The sweet spot is normally between 6% and 9%, as this is easy to maintain without being detrimental to other areas of the business and is enough to make a difference in driving more traffic to the business. Only you know how much you are willing to spend on marketing, but it is imperative that you allocate a budget for your marketing activities.

FINDING YOUR MARKETING BUDGET SWEET SPOT

A marketing budget is a necessity, but the size of this budget is dependent on your industry, location, time, and type of business. A company where I participated in their business accelerator program, found that after ten years of analysis, spending between 7% to 10% of gross revenue was the 'sweet spot' for them and gave them the best results. With my restaurants, I used to spend 2% to 3% of gross revenue, but I had a large variety of activities in my marketing mix. I was active on many social media channels with posts, a monthly email newsletter, local school directories, supermarket dockets, newspaper advertising, sponsorships, competitions, business networking events and community activism. I spent approximately five hours per week on time- rather than cost-intensive activities, which is why my budget had a lower cost value.

Benchmarking

In the years I have been teaching and consulting, I have found that many people do not know what benchmarking is. In our context, benchmarking is the process of comparing your business to other businesses in the same industry to assess its overall performance. Benchmarking is an important component of your plan as it tells you what you should be aiming for and where you are positioned in your industry. It is an amazing tool for checking industry standards, setting expectations and reviewing your performance in comparison to your peers. It is an efficient way to analyse profitability, productivity and growth opportunities.

Each industry has a unique set of key performance indicators (KPIs), which provide a standard for comparison. You can use this valuable information to compare and analyse how much is being spent on key operational areas of your business, such as marketing, rent, wages and cost of goods. This allows you to do an audit of your business and find areas that need attention, targeting them for improvement.

There are several benchmarking tools available that provide access to industry data and insights, including business and employment trends, key success factors, industry financial reports and key economic drivers. In Australia, the Australian Taxation Office releases this information on a regular basis. This data is collected from the financial returns that businesses submit every year. If you are unable to find this information online, ask your accountant to send you a report with the benchmarking breakdown details for your industry.

The objective of benchmarking is to measure your business' performance against the industry standards so that you can identify any areas in which your business is underperforming and make plans to improve.

BENCHMARKING MAKES BUSINESS SENSE

When I owned my first restaurant, I had no idea how much I should spend on wages, cost of goods sold or rent. There were times when I ran out of money and could not pay the bills. I did not know how I could pay the wages, let alone my own mortgage. I learned lots of ways to stretch every dollar and this became a major focus for me in all financial aspects of my life.

When I hired a business coach, she introduced me to benchmarking. I got the industry benchmark figures from my accountant and measured my restaurant's performance in the different areas of operations. This was transformational for me – I now had the data to see exactly where I could adjust and improve the business' bottom line.

Summary

In this chapter, we looked at why you need to have a marketing plan and marketing goals. We also learned how benchmarking can help you to improve your business by comparing it to measurable standards in your industry.

A marketing plan is essential when it comes to mapping out the strategies and activities that will grow your brand and generate sales, helping you promote products and services to meet the needs of your customers. Marketing plans should be working documents. Writing a plan and leaving it in a folder on the shelf or somewhere in the depths of your computer will not be of good use.

Marketing goals are specific items described in the marketing plan. They are the endpoints that you are striving towards with your marketing. Once you are clear about what you want to achieve, you can create objectives and strategies for how to reach them. Creating an action plan means you can more easily delegate work to your team.

Your budget and your plan work together. It is important to look at where you spend your marketing dollars and make sure they are spent wisely, giving you a good ROI. If you do not budget, you can easily waste money by spending it in the wrong places. To set the right budget, it is good to know the industry standard. Use benchmarking to find this out and to understand the measures that drive performance in your industry. Benchmarking will reveal the KPIs that you should measure your business against to identify areas for improvement. If you want to increase your business' bottom line, you need to know and compare your results to see where your business is under-performing. When you know this, you can work to improve your performance.

2

Resources

When you have access to the right tools, staff and information, you can increase your sales, improve your results, stay up to date with industry news and create useful assets to use for your business and marketing activities. These are the resources of your business.

With access to the internet, you have a wealth of resources available to you at the click of a button. Whatever you need is easily accessible at any time. Remember, a resource that was once relevant can become obsolete quickly and a new resource take its place. It is crucial to know where to get the latest news and best marketing resources, and it is good practice to maintain a marketing resource library of current and relevant information for all your marketing needs.

Pick resources that best fit your budget, preferences and style. Using templates creates consistency across different channels and platforms, as well as saving time, resources and money. Templates make it much easier to outsource the task to another team member. When you collate your templates, they become standard operating procedures for your marketing. It is good practice to have standard operating procedures for your marketing activities, sales, customer service and other areas of your business.

Staff are a valuable resource in any business. Hire well and train your staff to sell your products and services and to market the business. The more experienced and highly trained your staff are, the more of an investment in your business they become.

When you have systems in place, your operations flow more smoothly. A marketing system is one of your business' most valuable resources, and requires structure and careful planning. Later in this chapter I will give you some tips for how to create a system that fits your business needs.

RESOURCES CAN BE ANYTHING

Resources take many forms, from knowledge to connections. Anything you can use to reach an outcome is a resource.

When I was working my first full-time job, my manager told me that it is not important to remember every detail but to know where to look. This advice has served me well in my career and as a business owner. My contacts and connections are also valuable resources, as they are my team and save me time, money and stress. My external hard drive and cloud storage (I have lost many USBs and had computers die on me) are my most valuable resources, as they are the directories containing all the knowledge and information I've collected over the years.

Planners

When you have a lot of different campaigns and activities in your marketing mix, it can be difficult to know if campaigns overlap, or if the marketing mix is a good blend of concurrently running campaigns. A marketing planner is a calendar where you document every campaign and marketing activity in one location, which helps you get organised and balance your strategies and campaigns. Having a visual presentation makes it easier to see all your activities at once and fill in any gaps and/or quieter times of year. You can also see which campaigns are active and which are about to finish.

In your marketing planner, you want to give equal space to the campaign schedule and the detail of each campaign listed. This way you can view each month quickly, see your achievements so far and what you still want to accomplish. Then you can set goals for the next month. Using a planner makes it easier to remember when you need to start new activities in advance and add inspirations or notes to remember for current or future campaigns.

Mon	Tue	Wed	Thu	Fri	Sat	Sun	Goals and activities:
				1	2	3	
4	5	6	7	8	9	10	
11	12	13	14	15	16	17	
18	19	20	21	22	23	24	
25	26	27	28	29	30	31	

Using a marketing planner as a resource provides your business with a visual schedule for everyone to see. Studies have proven that writing down and seeing your goals regularly makes it 42% more likely that you will achieve them.[3] Having everything written down makes it much easier to delegate because you can see what's coming up and discuss with your team the work that needs to be done. A planner allows you to review the activities from previous months and remind you of the work that went into creating them and the results that were achieved.

A marketing planner is a great document to use to see everything in one place – holidays, events, promotions, advertising, competitions and other activities – and will empower you and your team through easy

---

3   Peter Economy Inc, 'This is the way you need to write down your goals for faster success' (28 February 2018), www.inc.com/peter-economy/this-is-way-you-need-to-write-down-your-goals-for-faster-success.html, accessed 20 May 2021

communication of marketing goals. Each item can be scheduled as an individual project with the time needed to create and implement it, as well as deadlines and appearing live.

There are many scheduling programmes available online that have this planning tool built in, like Hootsuite or Sendible. While these tools are useful for scheduling future posts to various social media channels, you can only see the results for the post activity, and this is not your overall marketing plan or marketing mix.

WRITE DOWN YOUR PLANS

In the early days of my second restaurant, I was asked what marketing activities and campaigns I was using. I had no idea what I had done and what was active. There was too much information in my head, with operations, finances and staff management to worry about. But I wanted to be more proactive and communicate clearly to my team what I was doing for the business. This was when I started using a marketing planner. It allowed everyone in the business to know what campaigns were active and which had expired in order to concentrate our efforts toward the overall goal of attracting customers.

Marketing plan templates

Without a template, things can get messy. There are many different marketing plan templates available online and it can be difficult to choose one. The type of template that is best depends on where you are in the cycle of your business. If you are just starting out, a standard plan template will include everything you need to know about marketing your business. These are available on government business websites and include all the aspects of marketing that you may not have not thought about and the main requirements for each of your planned activities.

When you have been in business longer, it is better to create yearly action plans, so you can take full advantage of the next twelve months and propel your business forward. An annual marketing action plan helps set your marketing on the right course to make your business goals a reality. Think of this as a high-level marketing plan that guides the direction of your goals and objectives, breaking them down into smaller projects and sections so that they can be delegated and implemented by the responsible member of your team.

Used correctly, a marketing plan template should be the engine that powers, steers and grows the success of your business. When you use a professional, tried and tested system, there is no need to reinvent the wheel. Templates are a good shortcut for creating your own beautiful, functional and effective marketing plan, but without the need to invest time or money in doing it all yourself.

FITTING A TEMPLATE TO YOUR NEEDS

I don't like creating a document from nothing, for something I have never done before. I never know what information is important to include. When I first started in business, I would spend hours searching for every template I could find on the internet, comparing them to see which was best to use. Some were basic and others so lengthy they were off-putting. By modifying one I liked, adding information I wanted and removing items that weren't relevant, I had a template that suited my requirements without having had to create it from scratch.

Standard operating procedures

When managing a business, standard operating procedures (SOPs) are necessary. Any templates you use or create can be added to your SOPs; these documents create the standards and values in your business, which tell everyone how to operate and be effective. As with your marketing planner, you should use templates to format your policies, procedures and processes of your marketing system.

The basics of a good marketing system are as follows:

- Policies that communicate the connection between the business' values and its day-to-day operations.

- Procedures that explain a specific action plan for carrying out a policy.

- Processes that tell staff how to deal with a situation and when, so they can be compliant with the standards and values that are required, an essential component of people management for your business.

Together, well-written policies, procedures and processes create the standards that help employers and managers to manage their marketing more effectively.[4]

When documenting policies, you should:

- Identify key processes and tasks in your marketing

- Develop SOPs for each process

- Allow your staff to contribute to the SOPs and regularly review the inclusions

- Ensure your policies are documented and accessible

- Make important procedures clearly visible

- Communicate your policies to your staff to help them understand them and why they are important

---

4   Business.gov.au, 'Policies, procedures and processes' (24 June 2020), https://business.gov.au/Risk-management/Risk-assessment-and-planning/Policies-procedures-and-processes, accessed 20 May 2021

- Educate staff on procedures that are specific to a certain role in the business

Good business practice is to have SOPs for your marketing, sales, customer service and other areas of your business. When you have these in place, your operations flow a lot more smoothly.

Your business may be subject to professional standards and codes of practice, so make sure your staff are aware of policies around warranties and refunds and compliance with codes of practice, your country's standards and consumer law. You, as the business owner, are ultimately responsible for everything that goes on in your business. Make sure you have well-developed policies and procedures to manage your legal risk and improve workforce morale, staff retention, job satisfaction and marketing activities.

CREATING YOUR POLICY DOCUMENTS

When my partner and I purchased the second restaurant, there were no documented policies, procedures or checklists. I had come from a franchise café that had loads of lists and procedures, but when I asked my staff where these were, they said they did not exist. They were expected to know what to do and asked questions if they didn't.

In the first month of taking over the business I created opening and closing checklists. These documents provided clarity about what tasks needed to be done and when. In the first two years, I created lots of SOPs including policies, procedures, checklists and processes, that went into separate folders for different areas of the business. These folders were: operational procedures, workplace health and safety, coffee SOPs, liquor license manual, staff management manual and money/marketing manual.

Years later, while working as a hospitality trainer, I was surprised to see restaurants and other hospitality businesses without these systems. I decided to create an online store to sell my folders as downloadable documents, so that a business could implement a system quickly rather than spending time creating it themselves.

Recruitment and training

Staff are a valuable asset to your business. In your recruitment, it is good to find out if a potential team member is best suited to a particular role, rather than hiring to fill a position. DISC behaviour profiling, which is based on how a person behaves in different environments, can be used to work out which team members are more comfortable with selling and who is best placed in your marketing team. It is useful to find out how a person tends to behave so you can see where they fit into your team and business operations. People who enjoy talking to customers are who you want on your sales team. People who are quieter, work autonomously and like structure are best for a marketing role. If you do not want to go to the expense of profiling each person, there is an easy way you can do it for yourself: ask them questions about how they behave in a workplace, look at their resume to see what roles they have held in the past and observe them in a sales role to see if they thrive in this situation and like talking to customers. Are they good at getting customers to spend more money by using upselling techniques?

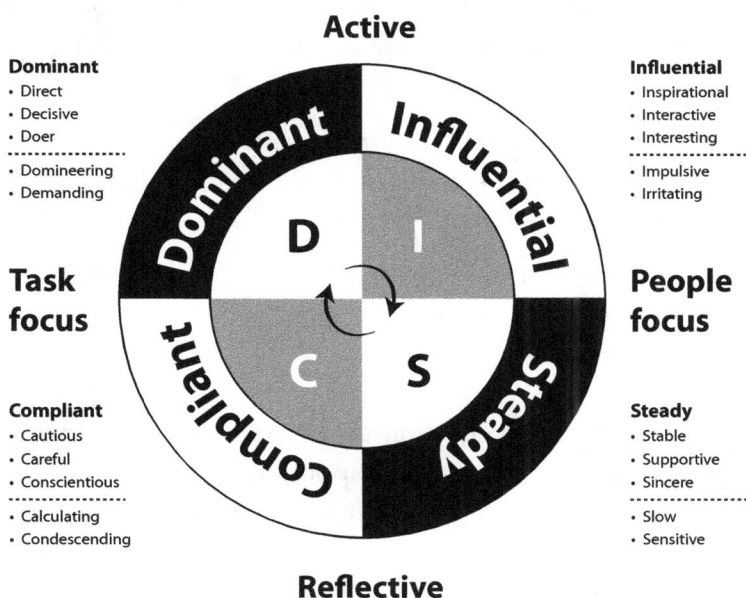

Active

Dominant
- Direct
- Decisive
- Doer
- - - - - - - - - - - -
- Domineering
- Demanding

Influential
- Inspirational
- Interactive
- Interesting
- - - - - - - - - - - -
- Impulsive
- Irritating

Task focus

People focus

Compliant
- Cautious
- Careful
- Conscientious
- - - - - - - - - - - -
- Calculating
- Condescending

Steady
- Stable
- Supportive
- Sincere
- - - - - - - - - - - -
- Slow
- Sensitive

Dominant — D
Influential — I
Compliant — C
Steady — S

Reflective

When you have the right type of person in a sales or marketing role, the next step is to train them to do the job effectively. Good training means higher productivity. It is an investment in your business and highly beneficial to every member of your team. Implementing training into your operations supports employee retention and avoids the expense of constant recruitment.

There are four key methods to train staff:

1. Classroom-based training programmes, where you train your staff.

2. Online training, where information is provided in the form of eLearning courses, webinars and videos.

3. Interactive training, which takes place in the workplace with simulations, scenarios, role play, quizzes and games.

4. On-the-job training, a highly effective method that requires participation in real activities that the job role requires.

Your staff are a reflection of you and how you run your business. If you are spontaneous and unpredictable, this is the how your staff will be at work by being reactive and needing constant direction. When you are professional, systematic and you train and develop your team, you will be rewarded with great sales, loyalty and profitability.

DEVELOPING YOUR STAFF

The staff at my restaurants were usually young, enthusiastic and employed for at least two years, which is great by hospitality standards. Most of them were in a Certificate III in Hospitality school-based traineeship or Certificate IV or Diploma of Leadership and Management traineeship, or they were Commercial Cookery apprentices. This was a great way to provide training to my team. My association with a training company provided all the theoretical information and, as the employer, the restaurant provided the practical training.

For the business, this partnership provided great opportunities. The staff were happier and grew in confidence as they had longer, regular hours, as well as job security and increased knowledge. During their time of employment, they achieved a qualification. I reduced my staff turnover, and the team members were more responsible, took pride in their job and had more initiative. This gave me, as the business owner, more freedom to enjoy my role of running the business, while also encouraging my staff's growth and development.

Creating the system

Once you have developed your marketing plan, marketing planner, action plans, SOPs and have a great team in place, you have begun to create your marketing system. Systems build successful businesses. They create a structure that provides consistency, direction and task management. A system gives you control, guides your priorities, creates processes, generates accountability and provides a way to find and measure your winning formulas.

The more systems you have in your business, the easier it will be for it to grow and develop its own identity outside of you and your passions. Having systems in every part of your business eliminates guesswork and staff know what to do and what their expectations are. When you have a system for something, you can apply any of the processes it contains repeatedly. In this way, systems reduce stress and save you time, resources and money.

The type of system you want to create is dependent on what your business needs. Your marketing system should be a compilation of your marketing strategies and SOPs including folders, checklists, policies, procedures, flowcharts and any other documents that are relevant to your marketing activities. Start by collecting and collating all of these, print them out and add them to your overall marketing manual/handbook/operating procedure and/or save them to an online folder to share with your team.

It is important to keep the system updated regularly so it remains current and relevant. The people who use these documents should be able to update them and keep them user-friendly and managed consistently. Creating a 'continuous improvement register' is a good way to track any changes and know what has been updated.

SYSTEMS EMPOWER STAFF

I love systems, as did my employees. In my second restaurant, I had SOP manuals for every department so that everyone knew the tasks that needed to be done, who was doing them and when they were complete. The manuals included opening and closing checklists, daily and weekly cleaning lists, work experience training checklists and even a 'don't know what to do list' (which included items like clearing and straightening tables/chairs, restocking, etc), instructions on how to open/close/clean machines and recipes for different blended drinks. Because they went through these manuals during their inductions, staff rarely asked questions at work because they could refer to them at any time.

The team loved the structure and felt empowered. Anyone who did not perform, did not last. Those that stayed, stayed for years and have often told me the restaurant was one of the best places they had worked.

Summary

In this chapter, we looked at the importance of having access to up-to-date resources, tools and information to improve your marketing, attract more customers to your business, grow your sales and increase profitability. Once you have the marketing plan, action plan and monthly/yearly planner completed, you will need a range of other templates and tools to manage activity across all the other components of your plan. These include SOPs for your marketing, sales, customer service, and other areas of your business. When you have these systems, your operations flow more smoothly.

Successful businesses are built on systems. An overall marketing system helps you get organised and create balanced strategies and campaigns. Good templates can help you create this system. Once it's established, you should implement it immediately in your marketing activities and update the documents regularly. Your staff are valuable to your business and are a part of your system. Recruit people who are suited to specific positions and train your staff to fulfil the needs of your business.

In the world of marketing, there are always new tools, tips, tricks, and trends to discover and incorporate into your marketing plan and strategies. You can easily pick the resources that best fit your budget, preferences and style. When you find what you need, you will be unstoppable in your marketing efforts.

3
Campaign Elements

Every marketing campaign is different, but there are some elements that are the same. In this chapter, we will look at the various elements you will use in your marketing system.

Overall, it is essential that you have clarity and consistency in how your business and/or brand is represented visually, from a graphic design and customer experience point of view. A style guide and style sheet will ensure consistency across all the materials you create; these documents are a vital part of your marketing system.

Using a blog or post template for your campaigns also creates consistency across different channels and platforms. The benefit of this type of template is that it provides uniformity, saves time, resources and money and you will always have a record of the campaign details to replicate or modify in the future. Templates also make it much easier to outsource the task to another team member and using it as a checklist for good management practices.

For blogs, images need to be royalty-free and tagged. Using an alt tag on your images helps the Google search bot index your image so it can be found on an image search and linked to your business. Tagging your posts with keywords and a geo location are ways to ensure that your post can be found via Google when searching by topic.

Tags, pixels and tracking codes are crucial for monitoring your online activity. Marketing is like fishing: by using an analytics platform to review your activity, you see exactly where the fish live. Tags, pixels and other tracking codes are your bait. When you know where the fish live and know what bait to use, you can land the fish on your hook much more easily. Once you have multiple templates, images, checklists, policies and procedures, it is time to collate everything into folders. Being able to easily find an image featured on your website or a blog that was written two years ago saves a lot of time, stress and worry. In the following sections, I will recommend a few different websites and programs I use, but there are many available in the online marketplace with new ones being created all the time and others disappearing.

PLANNING YOUR CAMPAIGNS

Like a holiday itinerary, my campaigns are thoroughly researched and documented in detail. I use a template and complete the required items. My blog templates have several sections including titles, descriptions, links, hashtags, meta descriptions, images, and article content. By having all the key elements in one place, I can relax and enjoy the process and know that there will always be a good outcome.

Style guides and sheets

Style guides and style sheets set the standards for all design work that is created for your business. A style guide is different to a style sheet. A style sheet is a one-page document containing basic information and brand requirements, which you can give to someone so that they can create something for you. For example, advertisers will usually provide the graphic design work for you but may need a few details from you to create it.

Your style guide, on the other hand, is detailed a rule-book that contains all the specifications for everything that plays a role in the look and feel of your business' brand. Everything from typography, colours, logos and imagery. It lets the user know exactly how you want to present your business brand to the world. Your style guide includes all your visual identity guidelines, which can include the following:

- Logos – the most important and recognisable element of your business' visual identity. The logo communicates who you are and what makes you a unique business. The logo often includes several components: the icon, the primary wordmark, different versions and colours of the logo.

- The favicon is a smaller icon that is based on the logo and is used for applications that fall below the minimum size required for identity and readability, like web page tabs.

- Colour details used in the branding – the Pantone value, CMYK, RGB and Hex values are required to replicate your brand assets and printing details.

- The typography and official fonts you use for your copy.

- The letterheads for the business in A4 size in both portrait and landscape orientations.

- The PowerPoint templates and slides you use for events and presentations.

- Business card designs.

- Your social media profile images, cover photos and any promotional images you have created with the sizes and pixels required for each platform you use.

- Any call-to-action banners, promotional flyers and video thumbnails you have created with the dimensions and designs/texts you use. Any landing pages, thank you pages, or other website page designs you have created.

By documenting all this information in your style guide, you will always be consistent and clear in your branding, design and content.

THE IMPORTANCE OF HAVING A STYLE GUIDE

In my first few businesses, I didn't have a style guide. I didn't even know what this document was until I started teaching a marketing class. This is when I discovered what a fantastic asset it was to have and I immediately created one for the businesses I was running at the same time. It has since become a valuable tool for all my branding requirements – I have found it convenient to have all the visual information and specific details in one file.

When I started creating some sales collateral for Maralytics, I was asked if I had a style guide. It was great to answer yes and provide this document with no need for explanations, searching to meet requests or stress. Once you have a style guide for your brand, you can take your business to the next level.

Blog and post templates

The content and images you use on every blog or social media post you write will be different, but the format should stay the same. Using a template for your blogs and social media posts helps you stay organised and have a consistent process and appearance. It is easiest to combine all the elements into one template that is suitable for every channel. There are certain elements required for each platform/channel, but generally these requirements are similar.

If you want to be seen as an expert in your industry, you need to be professional and be consistent. People notice inconsistency – little things missed, spelling errors, mistakes, formatting differences. By having a template, you can avoid or eliminate a vast majority of these before the content is uploaded or printed.

A template also helps with writers' block – if you find you are staring at a blank page, start by completing some sections in the template. This will help you get into the flow and words will soon start to fill the page.

A good blog post template includes:

- Date of creation and date posted
- Version number
- Title
- Title tag
- Website link and shortened link, call-to-action links and regular hashtags
- Description, meta description and social media descriptions
- The word count of the post and key phrase results

- Images used

- Purpose of post (eg awareness/evaluation/ purchase)

- Platforms posted to (eg website/Facebook/ Google My Business/Instagram/etc)

- Notes

- Article copy

By using a template document, regardless of what happens to the platform you will always have an original copy of every blog, article or social media post you create that you can keep in your back-up files. These files are good to have in the worst-case scenario that you lose your page or account on a platform and need to start again – if you have back-up copies, you can easily repost.

Another benefit of using templates is that it makes it much easier to outsource content creation and upload tasks to another team member, saving you time. You can also use the template for error-checking and training. When training a new staff member, having everything they need to know included on the template means they are less likely to get overwhelmed by the task or forget anything.

USING TEMPLATES ENSURES CONSISTENCY

I love using templates. My blog/social media post templates were the first thing I outsourced in my growing company. Using a template is the easiest way to ensure consistency across platforms. My first employee quickly became much better than I was at social media. I did it because I needed it to be done, not because I liked it. I found when I outsourced it, others did it better than me and I could be more productive elsewhere in moving the business towards its goals.

Images and tagging

Images are important as they capture your attention and tell a visual story. A post without an image may only attract a small number of views, and an article that contains only text is boring to read.

Many businesses use photos to showcase their products. It is important that these are good quality. If you are not good at taking photos, or they don't turn out the way you want, pay a professional photographer to take photos for you. This is a worthwhile investment as these images will become an asset if you are using, for example, Instagram to attract customers and entice your audience.

If you do not have products to showcase, or do not want to have your own photos, there are other options available. Do not use images from a Google search, most of these are subject to copyright and you can get in a lot of trouble if you do not get permission to use them from the image owner. Purchasing images is one possibility. To do this, you can contact the image owner directly or buy images through sites like Shutterstock or iStockphoto. These sites have millions of images available for purchase at a low cost. The benefit of buying an image from one of these sites is that it is more likely to be unique than free images and so is better for your branding. A design program like Canva enables you to create an exact layout that meets the requirements of the social media platform or document you want to publish. Canva has thousands of templates and a vast library of images that you can utilise for free, or you can pay Canva to help you create your content.

A free option is to use a royalty-free image. There are millions of free images available to download – some of the most popular sites are Pixabay, Pexels and Unsplash. The downside of using a free image is that you will most likely see this image being used by someone else, as these sites are unsurprisingly extremely popular.

When you upload your beautifully created image, there are three things you should do to get the most search engine optimisation (SEO) benefit and traction for the image:

1. Use an Alt tag, so Google can index it and find it on a search.

2. Add a geo tag so that the image will come up for people searching in your area.

3. Add a keyword and tag the image, so when a person enters a keyword in the search bar the

image will show up for them, enabling you to be found easily.

USING STOCK IMAGES TO CREATE CONTENT

When I first started doing my own social media posts and email newsletters, I used my own photos, as I thought taking anything off the internet was breaching copyright. A friend told me about Pixabay and Canva and I found a new world of content creation. My own skills are no match for a graphic designer, but I am skilled enough to find images to use for blog or social media posts, design a prototype flyer, or create a rough example of how I want something to look for a graphic designer to work from.

Tags, pixels, cookies and QR codes

The purpose of using tags, pixels and cookies is to increase your chances of being found and benefit from the ability to search and/or track who is following you. We use GPS to find the quickest route to a destination. These functions act like a GPS for your business, helping to find potential customers and vice versa. It is well worth getting to grips with them.

Tags and pixels are bits of code that your web developer adds to the backend of your website. There are many different types of tags as each one has a single purpose.

Google Tag Manager is a tag management system that allows you to configure and deploy tags. These include tags from Google Ads, Google Analytics, the LinkedIn insight tag, Twitter tag, Floodlight and other third-party tags. They help manage your online advertising and the digital footprint of your website.

A hashtag is a metadata tag comprising of a hash symbol followed by a word or phrase and is a form of user-generated tagging that can cross-reference content shared on a particular subject or theme. They are used to make the content or image more discoverable and clickable and are particularly popular on social media platforms. You can use them to search a subject, topic, location, event and many more trending items.

If there is one pixel that you must add to your website, it is the Facebook pixel. This pixel collects data that tracks conversions from your advertising on Facebook. It will also help to optimise your ads, build targeted audiences for future ads and remarket to people who have already acted on your website.

Internet cookies are ways for web browsers to track, personalise and save information about a specific user's activity on your website in their browsing session. Cookies track your browsing history and recognise when you visit a new website and are used for remarketing strategies in advertising.

QR codes are a quick and easy way to direct people to your website via their smartphones. You can have multiple QR codes for different purposes, for example sending traffic to a current promotion, enabling a customer to 'check in' to your business or sign up to a landing page.

WHAT YOU LIKE MOST MAY NOT BE THE MOST POPULAR

My website has over 100 blog articles and I wanted to know which articles have been viewed the most. I did a review on Google Analytics and when I got the results, I was surprised. The blogs I thought were awesome did not get as many views as I had anticipated. Do not go with what you think went well or what you liked the most, but always look at the numbers.

Folders

Folders, vaults or directories are a simple solution for storing your documents, images and other files you want to keep. Some folders will already exist on your computer, such as Documents, My Desktop and Downloads, but you can create more folders, and folders within folders, to allow for better organisation and grouping of files. If the number of files stored in a folder increases over time, it is a good idea to split the files into subfolders to make it easier to find the ones that you need. There is no perfect method for creating and organising your folders so don't worry too much about it but do make sure the folders you create have names that are unique and easy to understand.

THE BENEFIT OF FOLDERS

I love collecting information. For me, information is knowledge, and I have a vast library of documents on my external hard drive. Folders help me stay organised and be able to easily find a document, even years after I have last viewed it.

There are many cloud-based folder solutions available, such as Google Drive, Dropbox and OneDrive, that you can use. These solutions make your files accessible from any device in any location and you minimise the risk of losing things if your computer dies or your USB stick or hard drive gets corrupted. You can also share your folders and files with team members, friends and family, and password protect any folders you want to keep private.

When sharing folders, keep a back-up copy of the files in case of accidental corruption or problems with the shared folder. To control who has access to what information, limit sharing of each folder to only the relevant team members and remember to remove access quickly if someone leaves.

Summary

In this chapter, we have looked at the elements you need to run successful marketing campaigns. First, you need a consistent structure and approach and to have the right resources. Style guides and style sheets are the basis for your brand identity and keep all the visual components of your business consistent across all types of marketing. These set the standards for all the design work created for your business.

Templates for your blogs, articles and social media posts will help you to have a consistent content creation process in place and position yourself as an expert in your industry. Using quality images and tagging them is key to SEO and building awareness of your brand. Tracking is essential: using hashtags, pixels, cookies and QR codes makes it easier to track customer activity and make your business more discoverable and clickable. Having these resources set up is good for productivity and for replicating successful marketing campaigns; they can also drive more traffic to your website.

Store your documents, templates, images and any other files in clearly labelled folders. These are valuable items for your asset library and are the start of your marketing system.

Once you have all these elements in place, you have created the framework for a successful marketing system that will make it easier for you to scale your marketing and business activities.

PART TWO

IDEAS

Everyone wants more customers, but how do you get more customers quickly and without spending too much money? This is where you need to be creative with your ideas for attracting customers. Ideas do not arrive by accident. You can try to be more inventive by looking for inspiration and new ideas, but it is normal for tactics to grow stale.

Crafting great ideas for marketing campaigns is one of the biggest challenges for business owners and their teams. Great marketing ideas and activities can make a business memorable and inspire action, attracting customers to make a purchase. If you are not sure where to start, first consider what would be valuable to your customers. Marketing is a multi-layered process involving advertising, public relations, promotions and sales, through which your business is introduced and promoted to potential customers. Getting the word out about your business is one of the main ways to make sure it succeeds.

Implementing a social media ad or promotional campaign does not have to be expensive. If you are low on budget, with a small amount of creativity you can find methods that work and reach potential customers without breaking the bank. Once you determine which channels and activities provide the best ROI, you can invest more into those strategies. The most successful marketing activities use a range of opportunities, which all start from an idea and are then thoroughly planned, researched and executed.

There are various methods across online, digital and traditional marketing, with multiple channels that you can use to deliver your marketing activities. Some of these methods are in decline whereas others are going strong, with some ruling the marketing world. In the age of digital marketing, traditional marketing is not dead. Traditional marketing techniques still have value and relevance, especially when combined with digital strategies. The goal is to connect your products or business to your customers. The following chapters will provide an overview of some of the key methods you can use to generate ideas for your marketing activities and campaigns.

4

Online Activity

Your online activity is an important part of your business and needs to be recognised as such. Most people use a computer, smartphone or other device every day. If you want to find something, you go online to search for the answer. All the information you could want or need, is in your hands, all you need is a Wi-Fi connection to find it. In this world, listing your business online – having a website or profile where potential customers can find you – is a survival requirement. An online presence is a bare minimum, but there are ways to optimise it so that your customers can find you more easily.

Your business needs a 'storefront' that attracts customers. If a bricks-and-mortar business looks unattractive or unprofessional, potential customers will walk away. The same is true online. If your website looks clunky, is difficult to find or navigate, or takes a long time to load, you will quickly lose viewers. If your social media accounts, Google listing or other online profiles do not align, you won't be trusted. A business that has no consistency in brand or strategy may be perceived by potential customers as a reflection of the way it operates.

Do an online audit of your business to find out how it looks to potential customers. Ask a friend or family member to search your business and take notes of what they find and see, then create a list of what needs to be fixed. Most of this will be easy to update. If this is not your strength, ask or pay someone to do it for you. Remember, your online business is your digital storefront and the first impression your potential customers will have of you.

YOUR WEBSITE IS YOUR ONLINE STOREFRONT

In the last few years, I have been doing digital marketing consulting and have noticed that nearly every business I've talked to or worked with has lacked a strong profile online. Few small to medium-sized businesses take control of their online profile. Some consider it a low priority, while others do not know what they should be doing or how to do it. A business' website is its online storefront, with most people now using online searches to discover where to eat, shop and travel – not taking advantage of this is a missed opportunity.

Branding

Branding communicates the visual identity of your business to your customers and community, telling them what to expect and how you wish to be perceived. It provides recognition. It is a way to distinguish your business from your competitors. It clarifies what you offer and why you are the better choice.

First impressions count. What is the essence of your brand, what does it represent? Are you the face of the business, or does the business have its own identity? Conflating the two can be confusing for your customers. If you are the business, keep your online profiles professional. If you work in the business and the business has its own identity, keep it separate from your personal/professional profiles. Determine whether your brand relates to you personally, your business, or a product – clarify and define your brand(s). It is OK to personalise activity on the business' online profiles, as this creates connections, but be careful not to post about personal problems or troubles you may have – this could damage your reputation and/or turn off potential customers.

BRANDING MUST BE DISTINCT AND CONSISTENT

For example, Richard Branson is the founder of Virgin Airlines. His personal brand is distinctly different from his business brand. His personal brand is about him, his activities and his beliefs. Virgin Airlines has its own branding. Its products – from flight routes to cargo, pet shipping and gifts – are distinguished by the brand's signature red. Occasionally, Virgin Airlines uses Richard Branson to promote an element of the business, but the personal and business brands are kept separate.

Building a brand requires you to be clear on what your business does, who your customers are and what service/products you provide. A brand is much more than a cool logo or a well-placed advertisement. Creating a great brand requires a good process and strategy for generating experiential awareness. You can promote your brand through advertising, customer service, your reputation, promotional merchandise, and logo – all of these elements work together to create a unique professional profile. Consistency of brand is a sign of professionalism, stability, trust and dependability. Your branding provides a clear message about who you are as a business and how you want your customers to remember you.

An online audit of your business is again crucial, as consistency across all online and traditional platforms builds trust in and credibility for your brand. Having the same images and colours at every touchpoint reinforces the company's values in a visual way. Make sure that you use the same profile image/logo, banners and business name on every site as this is one of the biggest mistakes I see.

Google

You are who Google says you are. If you don't come up in the Google search results, how will customers find you? SEO is what determines whether or not you can be found online. When you use a search engine to look for something, you type in a single word or phrase, known as keywords. Using these keywords on your website and in your content will link your business to these search terms.

When you type a word into the search bar, notice the other suggestions it throws up – these suggestions will be common keywords, phrases, sentences or search terms related to the word you have used. Further down the search is a 'people also ask' section with questions, followed by a 'top stories' section linking to articles related to this keyword. At the bottom of the page are 'related searches' with other similar words and sentences, called long-tailed keywords. Long-tailed keywords are great to use as topics for writing articles and content, as these are the sentences people are putting into the search bar to find an answer, service or product. If you include these long-tailed keywords in your title or content, it will be found and be suggested to potential customers as an answer to their search query. Your website needs to have a site map, so that Google can index your business, pages and posts, making it easy for you to be found. Information and keywords connected to your business should be clearly presented and accessible for everyone.

When you use the Google search function, the first few items you're shown are usually ads. These will be clearly labelled 'Ad', in bold, as the first word of the listing. This is pay-per-click (PPC) Google Advertising and is one of the places that paid advertising is listed. If you are using a paid marketing strategy, be aware that every time someone clicks on your listing, you pay for this click, regardless of what the result is. There are other areas online where Google paid advertising is displayed, including text ads that appear at the top and bottom of the search results page. In Google Maps listings you will find businesses that have a physical presence in the surrounding areas near you. For your business to appear in this section, you need to complete your Google My Business profile and all its components.

Google My Business is a free tool that is essential for SEO and lets you manage how your business appears on Google Search and Maps. You can add your business name, location and hours, monitor and reply to customer reviews, add photos and learn where and how people are searching for you. Google reviews help build trust in your business and strengthen your online reputation, making potential customers more likely to purchase from you. Reviews make your products or services more attractive and can give your business a big credibility boost without you having to spend a dollar. They are included as part of your Google My Business tool, enabling you to compete on a level playing field with your direct competitors.

After the ads, backlinks are usually the next listings to appear in search results. A backlink is another website that links your business (and other websites) in their listings. The purpose of a backlink page is to attract traffic and build a database by linking to as many websites as possible on their site. These sites normally come high up in the search results because they have multiple businesses on one site, which encourages people to click. Examples of backlink websites include eBay and Groupon for selling products, Trip Advisor for the tourism industry and High Pages for services. Listing on these backlink sites is usually free, but you want to be in control of your listing so you can ensure it has the correct profile image, contact information and products/services, as these sites will be representing your brand. Businesses that run a backlink page import masses of information so they can get higher rankings. How your business looks on their page is not important to them; they want to increase traffic and use this information to collect a database and advertise directly to their customers. Your featured business is a small piece of their big puzzle.

You want to make sure that your business is listed in as many of the top search results for relevant keywords as possible. Ideally your own website would come up first, then your social media pages and, after that, your backlinks pages. Most importantly, you want to be at the top and not your competitors, so that you can attract those potential customers searching for a solution.

THE POWER OF POSITIVE REVIEWS

One of my favourite restaurants in Surfers Paradise, Costa D'Oro Restaurant & Pizzeria, uses TripAdvisor and Google Map reviews as its backlink partners. This strategy helps to attract customers to the venue. To date, it has over 1,068 reviews on TripAdvisor and over 1,360 Google reviews, both with average 4.5-star ratings. It uses a lot of other platforms like Quandoo, Zomato, OpenTable, The Fork, First Table, AGFG, Foursquare and others to maintain high search rankings on Google. For tourists who come to the Gold Coast, Queensland, Australia and search online for places to eat, Costa D'Oro Restaurant & Pizzeria will come up as one of the first options because of its backlinks and rankings.

Content writing

Content writing is a good way to provide information to your customers, increase brand awareness and gain credibility. People look online all the time; they may not need your product/service right now, but they might do at some time in the future. If you write articles and publish them regularly, you will find that when a customer needs your service, they will be more likely to look for you as they have been seeing your brand regularly, or your business is easily found when searching for a particular topic.

If you don't know what to write about, the first articles could be about your products/services. List all your products/services and say something interesting about each of them, their features and benefits. Investigate the problems your customers are facing and write an article about how your business solves them. Teach your audience something by telling them a relatable story.[5] Include keywords and look at all the long-tailed keyword search terms suggested by Google and include these as headlines for your blog/article. Another option is to use the website 'Answer The Public', where you can generate a long list of search terms for a certain topic or keyword and use these as headlines.

If you feel that you are not particularly good at writing, or do not like doing it, there are other options. One option is to purchase articles from authors who sell the rights to their work. These prewritten articles can be found using a private label rights (PLR) licence. Options to purchase an article kit start from $1.99 for thirteen articles varying from 250 to 1,500 words each. Another option is to outsource and hire someone to do the writing for you, or contract a digital marketing

---

5   N Patel, '8 (more) absolutely brilliant content marketing innovations from the world's best brands', Content Marketing Institute (11 July 2016), https://contentmarketinginstitute.com/2016/07/content-marketing-best-brands, accessed 20 May 2021

assistant. This can be an inexpensive option and you can find contractors on sites like Upwork or Fivrr.

Once you have your written article or blog, it is time to publish. Publish it first on your own website; this is your central hub where you want to attract traffic and direct all your enquiries to. Once it is live on your website, share the link via your social media accounts. You can then repurpose the content for your newsletter, email marketing campaigns or on blog sites like Blogger and Medium, as well as other professional sites depending on the industry. If you have written a longer article, you can repurpose it by splitting it into several smaller posts and create audio and/or video versions. One article can be utilised in many ways and is a great way for creating multiple streams of content online.

REGULAR UPDATES

Content writing is the main way you can educate your current and potential customers. I like to use image tips, short messages and quick-read blogs (1,000-word articles) to engage with my audience regularly. It is also a great way to answer frequently asked questions or solve 'how to' issues. In my marketing plan, I post on social media three times per week with regular content. Anything else that I am up to or that I want to share gets posted when it happens. With this strategy, there is a mix of both planned and scheduled content and I can also broadcast current news. This keeps my business relevant and provides consistency to my audience.

Scheduling

Uploading your content, whether that's social media posts or your email newsletter, to different platforms to maximise SEO reach is time consuming. If you are doing it yourself daily, you may not be using your time in the most valuable way. Scheduling allows you to streamline and automate these tasks and is a valuable component of your marketing system. You can do this yourself or outsource it.

There are different online scheduling tools available and their functions depend on who/what they integrate with. For instance, for scheduling of social media posts and blogs, I use Sendible, a great tool that integrates with multiple platforms enabling me to schedule one article to be posted on six social media platforms – Facebook, Instagram, Twitter, LinkedIn, Pinterest and Google My Business – in one action. You can tailor content to the exact specifications of each social media platform, making more efficient use of your time and ensuring that all-important consistency.

Trello is a useful tool for managing and scheduling your tasks and 'to do' list. It is great for delegating items to your team and keeping all the communication and documents related to a project in one place. Using Trello, you can clearly see and manage every task you and your team are working on and assign it a schedule and/or deadline.

According to Statista, more than 3.9 million people use email.[6] Email marketing is a valuable and cost-effective way to communicate – newsletters, direct marketing blasts, campaigns and autoresponders are just some of the ways you can reach your customers and clients. It is easy to send an email and does not cost money like posting a letter, and platforms like Active Campaign and Mailchimp are great for creating and scheduling emails to your customers.

It takes time to set up and train your team to use scheduling tools, but they are valuable resources for creating an efficient and transparent system. You will save time in the long run, be more consistent and be able to delegate tasks, allowing you to get on with everything else you need to do to run your business.

SCHEDULE IN ADVANCE

I schedule my regular content up to two months in advance. By having the work already done for the future, you can continue to operate as normal even in the case of unexpected events. For instance, when my virtual assistant was affected by several typhoons in a three-week period, her home was severely damaged and she was intermittently without electricity and internet. I did not have to worry about her work during this period. She had everything scheduled in

---

6   Statista, 'Number of e-mail users worldwide from 2017 to 2025' (February 2021), www.statista.com/statistics/255080/number-of-e-mail-users-worldwide, accessed 20 May 2021

advance and was up to date with her workload. She could take time off to sort out and manage her home situation without it affecting the online activities of my business. Both of us were happy, not stressed about the situation and able to continue a harmonious working relationship.

Data analysis tools

You need to collect data so you can analyse and act on what it's telling you. Using data tools within your marketing makes life a lot easier and there are various free and paid tools available to help you collect information and achieve your goals. Activity attracts customers, good marketing drives conversions. Data analysis tools help you figure out what you are doing wrong and right so that you can attract as many people as possible to your online profiles and give them a reason to convert.

There are plenty of options for tools, dashboards, platforms and specialised solutions for paid search, email, social, mobile and video, with new tools coming into the marketplace daily. The type of data you want to collect and the metrics you want to measure depends on your marketing goals and activities.

The Google Search Console gives you instant behaviour reports and you can run reports for as long as you like. Each report gives you information about where people click on your site, when they scroll, where users come from and more. Email marketing, social media and scheduling platforms can also provide you with data on digital footprint activity, and you can drill down into the demographics to distinguish your active target audiences.

A tool that can integrate your marketing campaigns and collect, aggregate and visually display your data in a way that makes sense to anyone viewing the information is hugely valuable. I developed Maralytics as I wanted a program that could provide performance reports on sales revenue, profit, ROI and customer acquisition for any type of marketing activity or channel. I wanted to accurately capture every sales transaction linked to a marketing campaign and have this import directly to the platform, and view that information in reports that would allow me to measure and evaluate the impact of my marketing campaigns on cashflow and business performance.

Data collection and visualisation provides you with the information you need to make intelligent and informed decisions and optimise your campaigns and marketing strategies. Using data analysis tools, attracting, tracking and converting customers is much easier. If you are not using these tools to run reports and adjust your activities accordingly, you could lose out on potential sales and/or waste your marketing budget.

USE TOOLS WHERE POSSIBLE

Marketing can easily be a full-time job, so I use tools wherever possible. I use templates for blogs and posts; I use platforms to upload, post and schedule blogs, content and newsletters; and I use data analysis tools to review the results of marketing activities. These tools allow me to delegate and outsource tasks to my team members and maximise efficiency while also helping to ensure consistency across platforms.

Summary

In this chapter, we looked at your online activity as an important component of your business. Listing your business online is essential for survival, but you also need to optimise your online presence so that your customers can find you easily. Building your online profile and having a consistent, strong digital presence creates trust and credibility, making your business more attractive to potential customers. This all starts with branding. Branding is your business' identity. What your business does/provides and who your customers are should be reflected in your branding.

Your business must come up in Google search results, as this is where most of your potential customers will find you – but remember, you are who Google says you are. Make sure that you are in control of your brand and how your business appears online. To get more and higher search result listings, create and post regular content such as blogs and articles. This is a smart way to provide information to your customers, gain credibility and answer frequently asked questions. You can use online tools and platforms to streamline content scheduling or task management. This will save time, as you can delegate to others in your team or outsource while ensuring consistency in your content across platforms.

Once you have active online content and advertising, the last and most important step of the process is to measure your results to gain insights and generate new ideas. When you know what is happening with and resulting from your activities, you will know where to spend more time, money and effort to get the best and most effective lasting results.

5
Digital Marketing

In this chapter, we'll look in more detail at the different digital marketing methods you can use to increase your business engagement online.

Digital marketing is a way of using the internet to reach customers. It is any form of marketing that takes place online. You can leverage various digital channels, such as search engines, social media, email other websites and platforms to connect with current and prospective customers online. Because of the wealth of options and strategies associated with digital marketing, you can get creative and experiment with a variety of marketing tactics on a budget.

Social media platforms can be used for paid advertising, building brand awareness and engaging with your customers as 'followers'. Audio podcasting can be used to provide listeners with knowledge and tell stories about your brand or business. Video can inform, demonstrate and take customers on a journey. Articles and blogs provide learning, credibility and information. Chatbots can fulfil service enquiries. These are some of the tactics you can explore when your business is active in the digital world.

As we've already touched on, it is vital that your business and brand has a digital presence. People now rely on the internet to search for and find out about businesses and services; by putting your business online, you make it easier to be found by and connect with your potential customers.

Digital marketing is different from traditional marketing in that it is not a one-sided conversation. It is participatory. People can engage directly with you and you can build relationships with them. They can impact your business in a way that is highly personalised and can provide instant feedback on service or direction for your business' future. With digital marketing you have tools like reporting dashboards to monitor the results of your campaigns within a platform or marketing channel, or you can use a tool like Maralytics to report and measure the results of multiple campaigns across different channels and for different types of marketing activities. In the past, you may have used a scattergun approach where you crossed your fingers and hoped that your message was received at the time your ideal customer was looking for you. Now you can know this for sure, as everything can be tracked, reported and measured inside digital platforms.

USING DIGITAL MARKETING TO PERSONALISE YOUR BUSINESS

With my second restaurant, I used email marketing to keep my customers engaged and remind them to keep coming back to dine with us. I first sent out a welcome campaign letter to introduce them to my mailing list. Then every year on their birthday I would send them good wishes and a special meal voucher. I sent monthly newsletters to keep customers up to date with events, activities, current promotions, specials and to introduce new team members. Every newsletter included a free item voucher that they could redeem within the coming month. The program I used for this was great as I could see how many people opened the emails, the bounce rate, the click-through rate and more. Looking at these reports alongside the voucher redemption reports, I had excellent knowledge of how I could drive more customers to the restaurant and increase traffic and sales.

Paid advertising

When you want to reach a wider audience or engage with new people, paid activities are a way to achieve this. In today's digital environment, you can be laser-focused in getting your message directly to your ideal customer to build your brand, increase sales and drive traffic to your website. For instance, Google Ads is a paid advertising service that displays ads high up on the Google search results list. It is based on the use of certain keywords, where more popular keywords are associated with a higher cost. In paying for these ads, you are buying the top slots on the Google search results pages. It is a fast and easy way to get directly in front of customers when they are searching for a solution that your business offers. You pay 'per click', so only when people actually click on your ad. From this click, they will be directed through to your website or can call you. If you create a good ad, you can use it to increase leads, conversions and sales, which can immediately turbo-charge your business.

There are other platforms that offer paid advertising and some are highly effective at directly and immediately reaching customers. Facebook, Instagram, LinkedIn, and YouTube are popular platforms where you can create and post ads and review the results. When you have the right ingredients for your ad campaign or message, these platforms can provide a big increase in conversions and sales with a low entry cost. You can effortlessly run multiple ads at the same time, all with different purposes and messages and targeted to different audiences. For example, you could run a set of highly targeted ads to reach a specific audience by matching the profile of your ideal target customer. This kind of paid advertising is a highly effective method to drive traffic to your website. You can run effective targeted ads with small amounts of money, but only you can determine your budget. The most important component of the ad is the length of time you run it for, not the amount you spend. It usually takes around one month to teach the algorithm who your ideal prospect is. If you can run an ad long term, it will be more successful in continuously attracting leads to your business.

PAID ADVERTISING INCREASES YOUR REACH

Whenever I would lead a digital marketing training workshop, I used paid advertising on Facebook. My database and social media followers were not enough to fill the event, so I needed to attract new people to fill the seats. I used a basic ad campaign with Facebook to boost the workshop event and spent $30 for a week. This was a small price to pay to ensure my events were full.

Affiliates and influencers

Affiliate and influencer marketing are powerful ways to attract your target audience and convert them into customers. It is important to know the differences between the two and how each strategy can increase your opportunities and improve your exposure. For instance, payment terms are quite different. An affiliate will receive a standard payment of a percentage of product sales, while an influencer can be compensated in several ways, such as a flat fee, payment per post or a free product.

Affiliate marketing is when you sell products on behalf of another business, or other websites sell your products for a commission. Affiliates often work with multiple businesses to ensure that the products they are selling get exposure. It is easy to measure the results from affiliate marketing as you can monitor the average order value, sales volume and site traffic generated by the affiliate. The purpose of affiliate marketing is lead generation and revenue growth, which is achieved through blogs, companies and publishers. Affiliate marketing is a simple way to increase revenue to your business, as you can sell more products or services than you currently offer, or have your own products sold by more businesses. Selling someone else's products and/or joining an affiliate programme can get you exclusive access to new content and special deals for your customers, and provide an additional stream of cashflow.

Influencer marketing involves partnering with influential people, such as celebrities, bloggers, media personalities and industry leaders to promote your products and services to their social media followers. Before smartphones and personal devices, the influencer marketing arena was limited to celebrities and a few dedicated bloggers. Social media influencers are now saturating the market, especially on Instagram and YouTube. When you collaborate with an influencer to mention or endorse your product on their social media channels, the hope is that their followers will buy from you. Influencers are viewed as experts or are popular within their niche; because of the high amount of trust social influencers have built with their following, recommendations from them serve as a form of social proof to your potential customers. Getting someone else to market your products/services to their followers and reach a wider audience is a good way to increase your brand awareness and increase traffic.

Measuring the results of influencer marketing is difficult because you need to capture the number of new followers, social media engagement, website traffic and lead generation that can be attributed to the influencer. If influencer marketing is the only method you are using, you can easily link any increases to the influencer, but if you are using multiple methods (as recommended) then it is harder to capture the results, but it is still a worthwhile addition to your marketing mix.

SELLING AFFILIATE PRODUCTS WITH A SIMILAR THEME

One of my friends is a Facebook expert and she provides Facebook marketing training. Her secondary business sells a range of products, and she uses affiliate marketing to earn extra money from her Facebook business page. She does not own, distribute or develop most of the products, but instead sells affiliate products and receives a commission from the sales that come from her site. These products are complementary to her brand – it is easier to sell an item from a range of products that are part of the same ecosystem, with a similar theme.

Video

Video has become important on every platform and channel and is essential to your social strategy. It is no longer one piece of your overall marketing plan, it hugely influences your reach and ability to connect with your audience. It is not hard to see why video is so popular. It is versatile and engaging; people like it because it is entertaining and easy to consume and gives your eyes a rest from reading. It provides a real-life glimpse of what is going on in your business and is easy to share across multiple platforms. When you add videos to your website or landing page, they increase conversion rates immensely. Videos are a faster method to increase engagement and awareness as part of your sales strategy, as they help customers make buying decisions easily.

Video has come to dominate social media. Research shows that on four of the top six social media channels, consumers watch video. Anyone with internet access can watch and produce video content. While there is a trend towards higher quality, professional video, anyone can hop on their mobile phone and create their own video in a few minutes. Video production is more cost-effective than ever.

If you are not creating video, you are unlikely to reach your engagement potential. In most cases, the simpler and rawer the video is, the more authentic the content seems. This authenticity matters to people. Live streaming is a great way to engage directly with your customers, as they can see what is happening in real life and communicate directly in real time. TikTok, Facebook Live and Instagram Live are some of the most popular options for using live video to market your business. These platforms have millions of users, so provide an easy, quick and effective way to get your message directly to a large audience.

USING LIVE VIDEO TO EXPRESS PERSONALITY

I have a friend who loves Facebook Live and uses it for birthday greetings. I laugh every time he appears in my newsfeed. He dresses up in different costumes and sings happy birthday to the person whose birthday it is that day. It is special, genuine and personal, a unique form of self-expression. Since starting the videos, his online exposure has grown exponentially and he is attracting followers both personally and professionally. I love to see how people are using live video to show what they are doing or to connect with the people who matter to them.

Chatbots

Chatbots are an example of automated messaging software that uses artificial intelligence (AI) to mimic written or spoken speech for the purpose of conversing or interacting with a real person. Bots are programmed to understand questions, provide answers and execute tasks. From a customer's perspective, they are a friendly and accessible time-saver. Rather than opening an app, making a phone call, or running a search, the customer can type in a message and get a response. As such, they are commonly used for customer service and you'll see them on webpages, apps and social media.[7]

It is easy to make and implement your own chatbot. You can start by greeting all new visitors to your Facebook page. If you are on Facebook, you probably already have the Facebook Messenger Bot, but may not have programmed it. By programming it, you can communicate with your customers at any time – and it is a lot cheaper than building a mobile app.

Chatbots can help you do many things in your business, tailored to its specific needs:

- **Talk to your enquirers:** When you visit a page and have a chat pop up, people are more likely to

---

7   P Cooper, 'The complete guide to using Facebook Messenger Bots for business', Hootsuite (9 May 2019), https://blog.hootsuite.com/facebook-messenger-bots-guide, accessed 20 May 2021

respond to the message than a marketing email. Responses are much higher with a call-to-action (CTA) button and will move down your marketing funnel.

- **Save time and money on customer service:** Customers hate waiting on hold. If they are asked the same questions repeatedly, this can irritate them and cause more upset. Bots can track and record the vital information from questions, so you can focus on the tasks the bot cannot do.

- **Greetings and lead selection:** Bots can greet customers and identify their needs by asking basic questions, so they can be put through a selection process that leads to your human sales team.

- **Ecommerce transactions:** Bots can sell. With the right script, bots can sell products and services within the conversation thread. They can also upsell by making suggestions at different points inside the thread.

- **Engage customers:** A bot can reach out personally. Bots retain information and can use that information to go the extra mile. A bot can offer relevant content at the right time and remind a customer that there are items in their shopping cart.[8]

---

8 P Cooper, 'The complete guide to using Facebook Messenger Bots for business', Hootsuite (9 May 2019), https://blog.hootsuite.com/facebook-messenger-bots-guide, accessed 20 May 2021

While hugely helpful, no bot can do everything. When you are designing your first bot, select one goal or case for the bot to handle. Keep it simple. Ultimately, bots are there to save time; a bot's success lies in automating the easiest parts of a conversation.

CHATBOTS ARE THE FUTURE

Chatbots are popping up on more websites with most having a general 'Can I help you?' type bot. During the COVID-19 pandemic, I experienced a chatbot that had replaced a real person and felt it was a fantastic customer resolution strategy.

I had booked flights and, due to COVID-19 travel restrictions, they were cancelled. It was impossible to call the airline, as there was no phone number and all service staff had been stood down. Initially, the chatbot collapsed during this period due to the volume of traffic and broken programming links.

After four months, I tried again. This time, the chatbot worked perfectly and created a ticket number to resolve my situation. I was given 100% credit for one of my flights, but a different amount for the second flight. I created another ticket number through the chatbot to enquire about the difference. This second ticket was again resolved quickly with an explanation that I had purchased the ticket in a different currency. The refund was for 100% credit in the original purchased currency and the difference was due to exchange rates having changed between the purchase date and credit date. I was happy with the explanation given. Most of this scenario was handled by the chatbot.

Chatbots are the future; they can collect information and use processes to achieve an outcome without taking up staff time.

Push notifications

Push notifications are messages sent directly to a customer's device. These are popular with big companies as they do not get caught in junk folders or spam filters and have a click-through rate that is double of email marketing.

They can be used as reminders or drive actions, such as promoting products or offers to increase sales, improve customer experience or send receipts.

Push notifications are direct communication with customers and so should be treated as a privilege. If value is not provided, the notification will be ignored or turned off and you may even lose the potential customer. Used well, they are effective at keeping users/customers engaged and conveying messages of urgency, so ensure you use good practices when writing push notifications. Remember that you will need to get the customer's permission to send these types of notifications.

One type of push notification is a message that pops up on a mobile device via an app. A business can send a notification at any time and customers do not have to be in the app or using their device to receive them.

SMS is another type of push marketing. When you want to send out a quick blast, for example promoting a special offer that is only available for a few hours, or send an appointment reminder, a text message will communicate that to your customers immediately, enabling them to act straight away.

Geo-marketing involves sending push notifications based on your potential customer's location. This works well for customers who are travelling or visiting a shopping centre, a location-based business or a tourist destination. You can attract new customers or existing customers to your business when they are in the area with a special offer that is sent out using the push notification strategy.

TIME YOUR PUSH NOTIFICATIONS

I can see on my phone which companies are using push notifications to engage with their customers. Recently I got a notification from Cudo telling me about an 'authentic Italian experience', which came at a suitable time, 12.04pm. If I had been out with someone and looking for somewhere to eat lunch, I would have considered taking up this recommendation.

Summary

In this chapter, we looked at digital marketing as a wide range of marketing methods that take place online. We explored the wealth of opportunities and strategies associated with it that allow you to be creative and experiment with a variety of marketing tactics on a budget.

We learned about how paid advertising can help connect your audience to your brand, generate sales and drive traffic to your website by using Google Ads or social media platforms, advertising functions. If you do not want to pay upfront for online advertising, we looked at how you can use affiliate marketing to have other businesses sell your products on your behalf, or have an influencer promote your product to their followers in exchange for a sales commission, a method that is becoming increasingly popular.

We learned that people love video, making it an important part of every platform and channel, dominating social media and the online world. By creating and sharing videos, you can engage more closely with your customer and communicate with them visually, giving them a glimpse of the 'real life' of your business.

We found out about one of the latest trends in marketing, chatbots, and how you can use them to achieve a high level of user engagement and solve customer problems in a time-efficient way, through scripted and automated interactions. As a first step, make sure you have your Facebook bot programmed and live.

Lastly, we learned about how you can use push notifications to promote your products in an automated way by sending short pop-up messages to a mobile device. Embracing this technology can help you communicate directly with potential customers.

6

Traditional Strategies

Traditional marketing refers to any type of marketing that is not carried out online. It is the oldest form of marketing and is also one of the most researched. Some marketers often lean toward these methods because they are tried and tested. We all encounter some sort of traditional marketing in everyday life, whether that's getting mail, reading a newspaper, listening to the radio or seeing an ad on the bus. This type of marketing includes activities that use traditional media such as television, radio, printed flyers/ads/business cards/promotions, billboards, live demonstrations and networking. Traditional marketing plays an important role in reaching local audiences.[9] An ad is normally

---

9   K Carmicheal, 'Traditional marketing vs digital marketing: why not both?', Hubspot (24 September 2019), https://blog.hubspot.com/marketing/traditional-marketing-vs-digital-marketing, accessed 20 May 2021

placed in the context where its audience will see, hear, or interact with it; if the advertising is in a physical form, it can be kept for a long period of time.

In traditional marketing methods, customers will notice you if you present your brand and message clearly. You need a good CTA or an offering to attract them to your business. As mentioned above, there are many types of traditional media you can use to communicate this, so make sure what you choose aligns with your marketing strategy and is consistent with your brand message. These types of activities generally have an unknown ROI but can return some impressive results.

If you have a bricks-and-mortar business, traditional marketing is equally as important as online marketing in driving traffic to your business. A good way to use traditional marketing is to get involved in your community; be an active member and provide support through donations, volunteering and sponsorships. This is a good way to get your name out there and benefit from word-of mouth – people talk and will remember your contribution.

USING VOUCHERS TO ATTRACT CUSTOMERS

With my second restaurant, for the first few years I relied on traditional marketing and had a range of campaigns in my marketing mix to attract more customers. When I first purchased the business, it was not doing well. One of the first advertising campaigns I implemented was a supermarket voucher with a 'buy one, get one free' offer. This coupon would attract more than 600 redemptions and sales of over $4,500 per month. It was a great strategy to attract customers to the business and keep them coming back as regular patrons.

Print media

Print marketing is a tried and tested traditional marketing strategy and one that provides credibility. Investing in print media tells customers that you are serious about your business and that you offer a valuable product or service. Potential customers are far more likely to trust your company when your marketing is presented in high-quality print. With printed materials, you know what to expect; they come across as authentic and trustworthy, creating positive engagement between the customer and the brand. Business cards, uniforms, promotional flyers, gift certificates, discount vouchers, signage, vehicle wraps and magnets, newspapers, magazines, books, brochures, the list goes on – these are all examples of print media. Many businesses forget to use print media as it is so basic, but it is still the most widely preferred method for special discounts and offers.

Print connects with potential customers because it is tangible. Unlike webpages and eBooks, print media has a longer lifespan. Brochures and leaflets can be picked up and put down and referred back to for as long as the holder has it. They can also be passed on to friends and colleagues, maximising the reach of campaigns. A flyer or business card will continue reminding the receiver of what it is promoting for as long as they hold on to it and keep looking at it. Being a physical reminder, this type of marketing provides the most lasting form of emotional connection, one that extends much longer than the initial contact, and provides value long term.

CTAs, links, QR codes and tracking codes are especially important aspects to include in print media, as they enable you to digitally track and measure the results of print marketing. You can then analyse the results to adjust and make your efforts more effective.

CREATE TANGIBLE BRANDING TOUCHPOINTS

In my second restaurant, I used many forms of print media in my branding touchpoints: the staff wore uniforms with logo; we had a rubber stamp with the restaurant's logo to stamp the serviettes, sandwich paper bags, take away boxes and anything else that could be stamped; I printed flyers with special offers that I distributed at events to attract people to the business. These methods were great for increasing brand exposure and attracting customers, as they were tangible reminders that we were there.

Community opportunities

Take advantage of opportunities to market your business within your local community. This is a way to engage with people in an active and nonintrusive way. You can find and engage with potential and existing customers in a location that isn't your business premises. Most people buy from businesses in their local surrounding area, usually within a short walk or drive. When you are an active member in your community, you will attract more customers to your business as people like to support local business and people they know personally. Following the law of reciprocity, community grows loyalty.

Being an active member of your community also drives innovation, authenticity and reinvention, as you are constantly striving to meet the immediate needs of your customers and will need to adapt and grow to keep up with their requirements. Good marketing always has your customers' needs as the focus.

You can engage in community marketing by providing donations, sponsorships and volunteer work opportunities. Speaking at local schools, mentoring students, networking and providing training programmes are other good ways to embed your business in the community. It's important that you are authentic; community engagement as a box-ticking exercise or attempts to push/sell your services will not be perceived as genuine and you can lose support. Make sure you have good reasons for any community marketing and that these align with your values.

To kick start your community marketing strategies, you need to identify key people. Forming a joint venture with a neighbouring business is a great way to cross-promote to both your customer databases. It is also nice to support each other and provide complementary offerings. Running a competition is another way you can work with other businesses to showcase each other's products and provide mutual benefit.

Being an active member in your community helps you stand out from your competitors and become known and trusted by the local people. If you can do this, lots of opportunities will open up to you and you will likely be asked to engage with and support the community further in a variety of ways. This is great for creating brand awareness and indirectly promoting your business.

HELPING YOUR COMMUNITY

During the five and a half years that I owned my second restaurant, I was a highly active member of the community and ran several initiatives with different groups in the vicinity. I employed teenagers through school-based traineeship programmes and work experience placements. I supported fundraising activities with donations. I sponsored charity programmes with merchandise sales and event fundraising. I provided gift vouchers to local schools for award presentations. I was a mentor and speaker at local high schools, giving talks on the hospitality industry and providing interview training. I did not consider these activities as part of my marketing strategy but instead saw them as community service. These activities were driven by my values and desire to help others and make a difference, rather than being the focus of my marketing.

TV and radio

The use of TV or radio (I would also include cinema and any media streaming apps in this category) for promotional purposes is called mass marketing, or marketing to the masses. This method is highly effective for achieving brand recognition, establishing credibility and delivering a simple message to a large audience. You can directly reach potential customers while they are watching or listening to a programme, a time when they are most willing to listen. You get to be creative and deliver a personal message about your business to a wide audience. Your advertisement can show and/or tell that audience about the benefits of your business/product/service or show prospective customers how your products are packaged and what they look like. Use this strategy when you want to broadcast to many people; it is not about building relationships with your customers, instead focus on appealing to as many people as possible.

To create an effective television or radio ad, it must be professionally produced. You will need to engage an agency to help create the campaign for you. The two other important elements are a good-quality script and a memorable story. Storytelling is a great way to make the viewer or listener feel something and inspire them to act; done well it can build a deep and strong connection that helps people understand why they should care. It is also a good way to add a human element to your marketing, which increases connection. You will be required to follow a code of practice when using these services; your advertisement must adhere to the rules and be accurate (which of course you will want it to be anyway).

STORYTELLING IS THE KEY TO MEMORABLE ADS

In my marketing classes as a trainer, one of my topics was storytelling. I studied advertising campaigns, and the ones that were most memorable had a story. I discovered that storytelling is the key to a successful film campaign. If you think about the ads that you remember, they always have a good story behind their messaging.

Experiential marketing

Experiential marketing is marketing with physical engagement, where you connect your business to a customer through a direct interaction in a real-life situation. You can show the potential customer what you offer and what you stand for, in person. With this type of marketing, you get to know what is going on in the marketplace, make important connections and create long-term partnerships. Common methods of experiential marketing include networking, expos, tradeshows and live events. Less well known but still effective methods include colouring-in competitions, themed staff dress-up days, cooking classes and business card draws.

Networking is one of the most popular ways of meeting people in a business community. It is a chance to trade information and create short and/or long-term relationships, potential partnerships and new opportunities. You can be noticed and stand out for your expertise and the services you offer. An interaction with one person could transform your business and result in unexpected breakthroughs, as likeminded people can share ideas that foster growth in their businesses and careers. You may have the opportunity to speak at a networking event. The benefit of being a speaker is that it gives you automatic credibility and positions you as an expert in your industry. When your customers or clients see you as an expert, they are more likely to do business with or buy from you. This can lead to new business opportunities and an increase in sales and new customers.

Expos, trade shows, conferences and seminars are good ways to directly engage with a wider range of consumers. At these events, a large volume of different businesses within one industry are on display, attracting a high number of people to one location for a short period of time. These events are a valuable opportunity to create connections with people in real life. Each event is unique and will attract different audiences, content and cultures.

Live events such as workshops and training classes are a great way to showcase your products or services directly to an audience. These events are participatory in nature, so you can engage and interact with your audience. You should include live events as a part your marketing plan, as they help build strong relationships with people in a way that is not always possible digitally/online and enable you to collect information and feedback on your marketing strategies and campaigns that can be used to improve your business.

THE VALUE OF FACE-TO-FACE

Meeting face-to-face enables you to connect with people and form a lasting relationship. A meeting I had with one lady had a huge impact on my life. We met at a ladies' networking lunch and had an instant rapport. We organised to meet for a coffee the following week to get to know each other more and see how we could work together.

I was a restaurant owner at the time and she worked for a training company. She introduced me to school-based and management traineeships, which transformed my business. After implementing many of these programmes, she encouraged me to get my own qualifications, which led me to my next career.

Promotional products

Promotional products are an incredibly powerful marketing tool, enabling you to connect with customers by engaging their senses. It is one of the only forms of marketing that allows customers to interact with a brand on a physical level. As promotional products are tangible, they often create a more memorable brand experience. A good promotional product can customise your brand message.

If you give people interesting and free branded items, they will remember you after the interaction. For example, brochures and promotional products help increase leads and sales and serve as constant reminders of you and your business. Examples of promotional products include pens, bottle openers, squeeze toys, highlighters, pens and sanitiser bottles. You can customise almost any item to suit a marketing campaign and make it more relevant to your brand or the specific focus of your campaign.

Promotional items can also be used as free gifts. If these are thoughtful, creative and useful they will make people happy and leave a good impression of the business being advertised. There are many new and innovative ways to remind your customers about the value you provide, and these items encourage repeat business and referrals.

Any size business can use promotional products. They are a cost-effective form of lead generation and often result in more sales with a good ROI. Customers tend to use these items and will give them to others instead of throwing them away. They are great for building branding awareness, visibility, customer loyalty and stronger relationships with your customers. Every marketing plan should include promotional products as a strategy. They can add value to any campaign and create a long-lasting, memorable experience.

USEFUL PROMOTIONAL PRODUCTS

I love going to trade expos to learn about the latest trends, find new ideas and get inspiration. I recently attended a hospitality expo to research what promotional products were given out, so I could see if there were any I could use in my business. It was interesting to discover what I thought was useful and what I considered a throw-away item. In my investigation, I found there was so much rubbish and money wasted on useless products.

The purpose of a promotional product is to give someone a reminder of your business. A branded water bottle at an expo is a waste of money, as you'll drink the water and throw the bottle away – there is no lasting reminder of the business. Items that I thought were cool included branded USB cable keyrings with iPhone/Android charger connections, branded sticky notes and branded keychain bottle openers. To me, these items were engaging and useful. I am still using them long after the event and, every time I do, I am reminded of the business whose branding they carry.

Summary

In this chapter, we learned that there is still an important role for traditional marketing methods, which remain current and are being used by many businesses today. It can be more interactive than digital marketing, makes it much easier to reach local audiences, and products/activities can often be kept active for a longer period. Traditional marketing uses several channels and strategies but usually involves some form of physical interaction with the customer.

TV and radio are best for getting your message out to larger audiences, delivering a simple message via sight and/or sound. This method gives instant credibility to your business; focus on increasing sales volume with this method, by broadcasting to as many people as possible.

Print marketing is tried and tested and is one of the most preferred methods for communicating special discounts and offers. Print connects with potential customers because it is tangible and creates a long-lasting emotional connection.

Getting involved in your local community generates customer loyalty and builds strong emotional bonds. As an active member of your community, you will be constantly meeting the immediate needs of local people and will need to adapt and grow to keep up; this drives innovation, authenticity and reinvention, keeping your business evolving.

Attending live events such as networking or trade shows is a good way to meet lots of potential customers in a short period, form partnerships and find new opportunities. Seminars and conferences allow you to engage directly with customers in ways that would not necessarily be possible through digital or online methods, building even stronger relationships.

Giving out free branded promotional products for your business creates brand awareness while leaving customers with a physical item that they will keep and thus be repeatedly reminded of your business.

Using any of these traditional marketing methods will contribute to reaching local audiences. Face-to-face and physical interaction makes it is easy to engage with people and for them to understand you and your business, which is one of the greatest benefits of traditional marketing over digital. It is familiar in its form, which makes it straightforward and effective for most people.

PART THREE

IMPLEMENT

In this part of the book, we will look at how the implementation of marketing can influence your business. Good implementation is critical for success, as it is where you put your strategies and planned activities into action.

First, we'll look at trends and sales cycles and how to take advantage of these to accelerate the impact of your marketing practices. Distinguishing each component of the sales cycle and being clear about which marketing activity is responsible for a sale gives you the knowledge and power to streamline your revenue. Connecting your sales results to your goals will help you make decisions in the business and determine how to move forward. We will also look at the 4Ps of marketing and how customer service, loyalty and referrals can affect your sales.

Your performance – ie your sales and profitability – shows you how well you are implementing your marketing system and is indicated by various metrics. Your sales figures are the most important set of numbers that you need to collect for your business. Without knowing how much you have sold in the past, it is difficult to predict accurately how much you will sell in the future and how you are performing at any given time. To have these metrics, you need to keep track of your sales and be able to attribute them to a marketing campaign, so that you can see if the campaign was effective. Evaluating your campaign success on the basis of sales performance will guide your future marketing strategies and move the business toward its goals. There are many different types of metrics you can collect and analyse; it is important that you measure the results that have an impact on your business goals.

7

Trends

Markets are ever-changing and you need to be able to move with the times to benefit from long-term business planning.[10] By keeping up with industry trends, you will have better ideas for your business and improve your marketing strategies in the long term. Trends are heavily influenced by customer habits and behaviours; even if your business is well-established in your industry, an up-to-date awareness of trends is important to show your customers that you remain relevant and are willing to evolve when needed. Monitoring changing trends in the market-place will also help you discover new opportunities

---

10 British Library, 'How to identify market trends for long-term business planning', Business & IP Centre (no date), www.bl.uk/business-and-ip-centre/articles/how-to-identify-market-trends-for-long-term-business-planning, accessed 20 May 2021

for additional sales revenue, for example by entering new markets and expanding your customer database when the time is right.

Trends do not come out of nowhere. Following key influencers on social media, reading industry publications, listening to podcasts, subscribing to blogs, utilising your network, using Google Trends and Google Alerts, monitoring competitors and speaking to your customers are all ways you can keep up with the changes that are constantly occurring. Trends come and go but being connected to what is going on in the world will help you gauge whether your business and strategies are on the right track.

KNOWING YOUR INDUSTRY'S TRENDS

While in the hospitality industry, I discovered by making a big mistake that there were trends I needed to follow. This mistake cost me dearly. I had come from a different industry and was not aware of the trends and cycles of shopping centres and seasonality.

In the first year at my second restaurant, I closed on all the public holidays. I had never worked on a public holiday, so I closed the restaurant. I learned an expensive lesson! The first public holiday the restaurant closed was Boxing Day (26 December). Afterwards, I found out Boxing Day is the second biggest revenue day of the year and I had missed out on over $5,500 of sales by being closed. Boxing Day is one of the few days (there are about three days of the year that reach this amount of revenue) that can boost your sales and profit.

In my second year, I opened every public holiday and could see the difference. It was good to have two years of experimenting with being open and closed. In my third year, I chose which days to stay open and knew the best ones to close. By experimenting and knowing the trends, I knew the days that were beneficial to my sales and profitability of my business.

Industry seasonality

Industry seasonality refers to the regular periodic fluctuations that occur in an industry, a predictable pattern of market activity in a particular season, quarter or month. If a predictable change or pattern recurs annually, this is seasonal. In Australia, examples include Christmas holidays, Easter holidays, summer stone fruit season, winter snow skiing, flower blooming and school holidays, but can also include any other times of year that are predictably busy or quiet periods for your business.[11]

Seasonal opportunities are enormous, as they usually come at the most commercially critical times of the year. A business can earn most of its income during a small number of weeks or months during a calendar year and can make enough money during these periods to sustain operations at quieter times of year. Be prepared, embrace seasonal activities and take

---

11 L Ross, 'The impact of seasonality: 5 tips for a successful seasonal marketing campaign', Invesp (13 August 2018), www.invespcro. com/blog/seasonal-marketing-campaign, accessed 20 May 2021

advantage of them by having the right products on offer in the right place at the right time. Be flexible and, as we learned earlier, up to date with trends, so that you are able to adjust to any changes and can take advantage of new opportunities to make more money.

No matter what time of year is most profitable for your business, it is important to be proactive about identifying your seasonal trends and acting on them. Start each year by drawing up a calendar for your business and scheduling your busy times, following your industry's seasonality. This is one of the easiest ways to fill up your marketing plan with opportunities you can take advantage of with little effort.

FINDING YOUR SEASONAL PATTERN

With my second restaurant being located in a shopping centre, I was impacted by the seasonality of the retail industry. The shopping centre and stores heavily promoted the holiday seasons. Christmas and school summer holidays were peak periods and sales increased by 40% during December and January. Customers also behaved differently. More people were walking around and there were decorations and promotions everywhere. Once I got to know this pattern, I could order more stock, train and roster staff according to the peak times and optimise my business' performance. I learned that the Thursday before Christmas Day was my peak trading day of the year, followed by Boxing Day. Knowing this information made it simple for me to predict the future. There is a huge difference in having sales of $2,000 on an average day and having $5,500 in sales on a peak day.

Regular events

Regular events go hand in hand with seasonality; they are recurring but shorter-term 'special' sales periods. You can connect with customers through hosting regular events and may see changes in customer purchasing habits. Events may require unique content, perfect campaign execution and excellent timing – all this needs to be considered ahead of time.

Observe the stores in your local shopping centres and note their marketing activities. They will always be promoting the next event to attract more customers. Note the dates of these regular events. When you know when these are occurring, you can plan campaigns or activities a long way into the future and be ready to implement or update the theme at any time to take advantage of emerging trends.

Some regular events that can be added to your marketing planner are:

- **January:** New Year's Day on 1 January signals a fresh start

- **February:** With Valentine's Day on 14 February, love and romance are the themes for this month

- **March:** You can tie activities into St Patrick's Day celebrations (17 March)

- **April:** April Fool's Day is on 1 April, and Good Friday and Easter typically fall in April (though they can also be in March some years)

- **May:** Opportunities include Star Wars Day ('May the fourth be with you') and Mother's Day (in some countries, Mother's Day is celebrated in March)

- **June:** This month marks the halfway point in the year and the changing of seasons. In Australia, it is tax time

- **July:** American Independence Day is 4 July

- **August:** International Beer Day is 6 August

- **September:** Father's Day is the first Sunday of the month (in some countries, Father's Day is celebrated in June)

- **October:** Halloween on 31 October offers an opportunity to dress up

- **November:** The Day of the Dead is 2 November, Thanksgiving is celebrated at the end of the month, followed by Black Friday and Cyber Monday

- **December:** With Christmas and other holidays, this is the season for gift giving

Wherever in the world you are located, you will find these types of regular events. Some may be specific to your country, state, community, culture or faith. Add them all into your yearly planner so you know when to use them as to promote a sale or event in your business. Take advantage of the hype your customers will already be used to surrounding these times and events.

CELEBRATING SEASONAL EVENTS

In all my restaurants, Valentine's Day, Easter, Mother's Day, Father's Day and Halloween were regular events where we dressed up in costumes, gave away free chocolates or flowers, set special menu items and decorated the restaurant. We used these events as a reason to give our customers a distinct experience that differed from the normal routine.

Special events

Special events are considered 'special' because they are one-offs that fall outside of the normal business activity, industry seasonality and regular events. This type of event is an opportunity to spice up your marketing activities with fun ideas, to entertain your customers while driving extra traffic to your business. It is generally social rather than business-led in nature and can be aligned with your personal beliefs and values.

Parties and celebrations, brand communication events, charity/non-profit fundraisers, community and local council entertainment, parades/festivals, demonstrations and public events are all opportunities you can take advantage of to create special events. For instance, drawing on some of the traditional marketing techniques we discussed earlier, you might consider offering sponsorships within the community, running competitions, or collaborating with another business, which can increase sales for both of you, and in a more meaningful way. You could try one-off activities to attract more customers and experiment with promoting your business, brand, product or service. Any special event is an opportunity to increase your exposure, build recognition, widen your circles and generate more revenue. You get to engage with your customers in a less formal setting and potentially have them spend more money. These opportunities create stronger connections to your community and give your staff a reason to be more engaged, as it is a break from the daily grind. New products, demonstrating your values and showcasing innovative ideas are all great reasons to create a special event where you can show off and attract the attention of both existing and potential customers.

When you create a special event, you are making an emotional connection with your people. You are providing opportunities for everyone to engage on a more personal level and deepen the emotional ties your customers have with your business.

TURNING YOUR TEAM'S PASSIONS INTO EVENTS

In all my restaurants, I loved hosting charity events and supporting causes that were important to me and my team. One of my staff members was extremely passionate about looking after animals and she wanted to do something in the restaurant to promote her cause. I organised a merchandise box from the RSPCA to fundraise and had vegan specials for the entire week. It became a tradition that I continued for many years across several venues.

Technology trends

When running a business, it is important to connect with your customers in as many ways as possible. If you do not adapt and keep up, you will miss out and struggle to stay viable. It does not matter what industry your business is in or what products or services you offer, technology trends cannot be ignored. Not too long ago I was using directories like Yellow Pages, newspapers, radio and flyers to promote my business. Until recently, a website and Facebook page were enough of an online presence – but the digital landscape is evolving quickly and it is imperative to keep up with new opportunities as they arise.

Social media is huge and varied. It is helpful to know what platforms your customers are on and to coordinate your activities on those platforms to have the impact you want. As covered in Chapter 5, chatbots are AI software that offer personalised, focused interactions can be used for thousands of different business tasks. Video marketing allows you to interact with your audience, for example through live streaming. Content marketing can connect your business to customer search queries and help develop brand awareness among potential customers. Email marketing remains a major channel for direct communication, but it has evolved so that generic marketing emails are no longer as effective as they used to be. Automation and personalisation can motivate action from your customers.

Interactive content is a new and highly effective way to offer people a more immersive and engaging experience, making them feel more connected to the company. This can be done through quizzes and polls, augmented reality ads, 360-degree videos and voice devices. Adopting a voice search strategy will help you earn a coveted position in Google rankings, as fewer businesses are using it. Geo-targeting delivers your ads to an audience in a specified geographical area, and messenger marketing enables you to reach customers directly with short, personalised texts with a high engagement return.

By using an omnichannel approach across multiple platforms, including email, apps, and social media, your business can connect with customers at more digital touchpoints. You can offer an enhanced user experience and generate better results. Customer retention, order value and purchase frequency will be higher when you use multiple channels and take advantage of technology trends.

TRACK AND MEASURE YOUR MARKETING ACTIVITIES AUTOMATICALLY

Since the global financial crisis in 2008, there have been huge changes in technology. Smart phones, social media and digital advertising have changed the marketing landscape since 2010, the year I got the idea for my business when I wanted to track and measure my restaurant's marketing activities automatically. However, with the software available at the time, I could only collect and report the results manually.

This was a problem I saw other businesses had as well, and I wanted to find a solution for it. As technology advanced, I discovered how to develop a software program that can do everything I wanted. I founded Maralytics in 2016.

Advertising your business is now more targeted as you can be specific about the people you want to send your message to. Technology makes it easier to promote your business and with more success.

Industry trends

It is essential to keep an eye on trends that are specific to your industry. Every industry has undergone tremendous changes and disruptions over the last two decades. It is essential for your short-term survival and long-term competitiveness that you understand the current and emerging trends in your industry.

Look at the key trends that have shaped your industry, as well as any changes that are occurring or upcoming, and see what direction the industry is heading in. This will enable you to update and tailor your services to take advantage of current trends and remain relevant and competitive. For example, new technology solutions can streamline business operations and attract more customers; sanitation and cleanliness protocols have evolved as a result of the COVID-19 pandemic; and concern for the environment has encouraged more businesses to source local products and find ways to be more sustainable.

One way to identify the latest trends in your industry is to use Google Trends, which will tell you what the broader search or seasonality habits are over a given time frame. You can also do research on blogs, news sites and forums to gather data and review industry reports and publications to pinpoint opportunities. It is a good idea to follow prominent influencers within your industry, as they will let you know what is around the corner.

For instance, there are several trends affecting the hospitality industry today. Many restaurants are using Instagram to showcase menu items. The popularity of delivery channels like Uber Eats and Menulog is making interactive menus where your customer can see exactly what their meal will look like with recommended add-ons and upsells a must.

USING INSTAGRAM TO ATTRACT NEW CUSTOMERS

In the hospitality industry, Instagram is becoming increasingly popular. It allows restaurants to upload beautiful images and videos to connect with their customers and attract new ones. One of my favourite cafés on the Gold Coast has used this to grow its business. At the time of writing their account has over 53,800 followers, and the café, which is tucked away and not visible to passers-by, is always full. It is a destination venue. It has taken advantage of the Instagram trend within the industry by posting pictures of its pastry creations, such as Iced Vovo eclairs, twice-baked Snickers croissants and Nutella bombs. It is reaping the rewards, with a remarkably successful business.

Summary

In this chapter, we looked at how keeping up with the latest trends in technology and in your industry provides you with fresh ideas for marketing your business. You need to move with the times and find new ways to influence customers and improve your long-term business outlook. Fads come and go but crafting an ongoing strategy that takes advantage of trends to meet the need of your business is critical.

Seasonality relates to predictable patterns of activity throughout the calendar year. Often a business can earn a large proportion of its annual income during a small period of time, which can sustain it for the rest of the year. It is important to know about any relevant sales cycles and community events, adjust to any changes and take advantage of opportunities that arise. Regular and special events often encourage customers to behave differently and provide a different way to connect with them; these events can be specific to your country, culture or community.

Keeping abreast of industry trends help you to evolve your business and remain competitive, while awareness of technology trends will suggest new ways to interact and engage with your customers and make them feel more connected to the business. Analysing trends improves your marketing, as you can identify patterns in your industry and take advantage of these to make better decisions around your long-term marketing strategy.

8
Sales

Sales and marketing are two separate areas in the business, but both relate to lead generation and revenue. Sales activities cover everything that directly leads to the selling of goods and services, whereas marketing is the process of getting people interested in the products and services being sold.

When running a business, you will record your sales revenue so you can report on your financial performance, but this type of reporting has nothing to do with your business or marketing goals. You want to connect your sales results to your goals so you can make decisions about how to move the business forward. As part of the marketing cycle, you can rate your marketing activities by analysing the sales that have directly resulted from the marketing campaigns you have implemented.

The 4Ps of marketing can differentiate you from your competition. Having a clearly defined sales cycle provides your business with reference points that allow you to better organise your pipeline, prioritise your leads and evaluate your sales efforts, and you can see exactly where the customer is inside the cycle.

Customer service is the support you offer to your customers both before and after they buy and use your products or services and is an important aspect of your business operations. Prioritising customer service helps you attract and retain loyal customers and so can impact your bottom line.

The easiest and most predictable source of new revenue is your existing customers, those who already know your business and have bought from you before. Selling to existing customers leads to higher profits – it is less focused on price because they already know and trust you. The best source of new business is a referral from a satisfied customer, this is one of the most powerful selling and marketing tools available and something that you don't have to do any work for. It's great when someone who has been to your business or experienced your service recommends you to a new customer.

TRACKING SALES FROM YOUR MARKETING CAMPAIGNS

In my restaurants, every sale that came from a marketing campaign was tracked and measured. Every discount voucher presented would be stapled to a printed receipt of the transaction. At the end of the day, during the register reconciliation, the vouchers and matching receipts were collated, and the totals were added to a spreadsheet that collected the results from each marketing campaign. At the end of the month, the results were tallied and added to a separate spreadsheet. This second spreadsheet measured the month or total results for every campaign, with details of the sales revenue, vouchers redeemed and the cost of campaign, with formulas for calculating results.
At a glance, I could view campaign sales, profit, ROI, customers and costs and compare the results to those achieved via other channels or at different times. I used these insights to create future campaigns, negotiate with advertising suppliers, make business decisions and streamline marketing activities.

The 4Ps of marketing

The 4Ps of marketing (product, price, place and promotion) are essential for selling and promoting your products or services. They are often constrained by internal and external factors in the overall business environment and interact significantly with each other. The concept that you could control marketing elements was created in the 1960s by Neil Borden,[12] who demonstrated the ways that companies could use advertising tactics to engage their customers and overcome the barriers to purchasing. Jerome McCarthy distilled Borden's work further to generate the four-element framework: Product, Price, Promotion and Place.[13] The idea is that if you implement all of the 4Ps into your sales strategy, keeping the customer as the focus, you will generate more sales.[14]

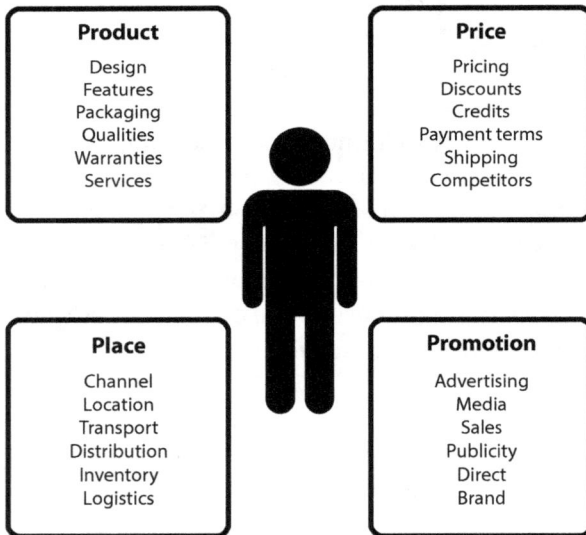

Product

Design
Features
Packaging
Qualities
Warranties
Services

Price

Pricing
Discounts
Credits
Payment terms
Shipping
Competitors

Place

Channel
Location
Transport
Distribution
Inventory
Logistics

Promotion

Advertising
Media
Sales
Publicity
Direct
Brand

---

12 N H Borden, 'The concept of the Marketing Mix', *Journal of Advertising Research* (1964), June, pp 2–7

13 E Constantinides, 'The Marketing Mix Revisited: Towards the 21st century marketing' (2006), *Journal of Marketing Management*, vol 22, https://doi.org/10.1362/026725706776861190), accessed 17 August 2021; Pdf of article can be downloaded here: intranet.fucape.br/uploads/MATERIAIS_AULAS/25112-8.pdf

14 A Twin, 'The 4 Ps', Investopedia (19 February 2021), www.investopedia.com/terms/f/four-ps.asp, accessed 20 May 2021

1. **Product:** This is what you sell – physical goods or services.

2. **Price:** This is how much you charge, which impacts your customer's view of your brand.

3. **Place:** This is where you promote your product or service, and where your ideal customers go to find information about your industry.

4. **Promotion:** This is how your customers find you, what strategies you use to attract customers and how effective they are.[15]

All 4Ps need to be considered in relation to one another, and it does not matter in what order. Integrating them into your sales strategy helps you define the elements you need to create a successful marketing offer. Essentially, it is about putting the right product in the right place, at the right price, in the right way.

RESEARCHING YOUR MARKET

I used to do a lot of research for all my restaurant's menu prices, and it was time well spent. It is much easier now, as most places have their menus on their website. Before the online revolution, I would do research by taking photos of competitor menus, but I often got strange looks and questions. When designing my menu, my main rule was, how much would I pay for

---

15 N Patel, 'The 4 Ps of marketing: what you need to know (with examples)', NeilPatel.com (no date), https://neilpatel.com/blog/4-ps-of-marketing, accessed 20 May 2021

it, given this location and venue? My second restaurant was in a shopping centre, and my prices needed to be reasonable to attract as many customers as possible. I wanted to produce a quality meal for a reasonable price, so customers could come in as often as they wanted.

Sales cycle

Successful sales are rarely the result of random actions and activities. Generally, a business that sees consistent sales success offers their salespeople some degree of guidance. Your business needs a defined process that gives staff a detailed pathway, as suggested by Meg Prater so they can see where they are in the sales cycle.[16]

It is in your business' best interest to have a sales cycle in place – a set of specific actions that are followed to gain a new customer. This provides your business with reference points and, if there is a break or pause in the cycle, you can investigate and objectively evaluate your sales efforts to know what your team are doing, what works well, what has gone right/wrong, and what happens if staff do not follow the cycle. Staff should understand what they need to do and when and the sales cycle shows where the customer is in their buying journey. You can use this structure to evaluate your sales staff's performance and where in the cycle they are strong or need help.

16 M Prater, 'The sales cycle: the backbone of a successful sales effort', Hubspot (19 March 2020), https://blog.hubspot.com/sales/sales-cycle, accessed 20 May 2021

According to Prater,[17] the seven stages of a sales cycle are:

1. **Prospect:** This is the potential customer who is looking for a solution to meet their needs.

2. **Connect:** When your prospect has approached you, or you have found them, it is time to connect and engage with them.

3. **Qualify:** This is when the prospect evaluates your business to see if it meets their needs, or when you ask them questions to see if you can fulfil their requests.

4. **Present:** This is your presentation or pitch about your products/services.

5. **Objections:** Your prospect may have some questions or concerns.

---

17 M Prater, 'The sales cycle: the backbone of a successful sales effort', Hubspot (19 March 2020), https://blog.hubspot.com/sales/sales-cycle, accessed 20 May 2021

6. **Close:** You ask the prospect to buy or sign up and complete the sale. If their response is no, you may need to return to an earlier step in the cycle.

7. **Follow up and generate referrals:** There are always opportunities to refer, get referrals, new business connections, cross-sell and upsell to nurture the relationship and drive revenue.

When you follow every step in the sales cycle, you can streamline your sales activity to increase your revenue and improve customer experience. The sales cycle provides an overall outline for what you should be doing in your business: finding potential customers, closing the sale and retaining clients for repeat business and referrals in the future.

DEFINING YOUR SALES CYCLE

Every business has its own sales cycle. In my last two restaurants, I had a clearly defined sales cycle. Prospecting was done by researching and experimenting with my marketing campaign mix. Connecting was achieved via the marketing activities, such as advertising, promotions and competitions. Qualifying involved an appealing voucher or redemption offer. Presentation was the free item given as part of the voucher offer. Objections would be customer complaints, which I handled by keeping customers happy. Close was the sale. I also offered an upsell or additional product strategy and trained my team on how to maximise every customer spend. Follow-up was our loyalty programme. We recorded customers' details on a database, so we could use email marketing campaigns to send out offers to entice them back to the restaurant to spend more money.

Customer service

Customer service is the support you offer to your customers both before and after they buy and use your products or services. It is what ensures they have an easy and enjoyable experience with you. Prioritising customer service will help you to attract and retain loyal customers and grow your business.[18]

Customer service can take place via email, web, text message, social media, support agents, help desks or telephone support, among other options. Many companies are starting to provide self-service support, like chatbots and directories, to enable customers to find their own answers at any time. Customer service is about more than answering queries, however, it is an important part of the promise your business makes to its customers.

It is well known that it is cheaper to keep existing customers than to find new ones. According to Invesp, 'Existing customers are 50% more likely to try new products and spend 31% more, when compared

---

18 Salesforce, 'Overview: what is customer service?', (no date), www.salesforce.com/products/service-cloud/what-is-customer-service, accessed 20 May 2021

to new customers.'[19] Lack of, or worse, bad customer service, is a key driver of loss and churn of regular customers; most customers leave a business because they have had a negative experience.

With today's technology, it is critical to meet customers' expectations as a business' reputation can be easily damaged. Negative Google reviews or comments on social media platforms can put off prospective customers; these can quickly reach large audiences and leave a permanent mark on your digital presence. How you handle negative reviews and comments is a component of your customer service; responding in a professional and empathetic manner will be viewed as good customer service.

There are eight ways you can provide excellent customer service in your business:

1. **Work as a team:** Everyone in the business should be part of the customer service process.

2. **Listen:** Take time to understand what the customer wants and needs.

3. **Be friendly:** Smiling is free and showing personality is encouraged.

4. **Be honest:** Always tell the truth – you cannot know everything and no-one likes being lied to.

---

19 K Saleh, 'Customer acquisition vs retention costs – statistics and trends', Invesp (16 March 2018), www.invespcro.com/blog/ customer-acquisition-retention, accessed 20 May 2021

5. **Practise empathy:** Put yourself in the customer's shoes, especially in tough situations – your customer will appreciate it.

6. **Know your product:** Knowing all the details about what you are offering makes it easier to answer questions and sell.

7. **Timeliness:** People hate waiting and want to be serviced as quickly and efficiently as possible.

8. **Improve processes:** If you are seeing the same complaint repeatedly, there is an issue that needs to be fixed as soon as possible.

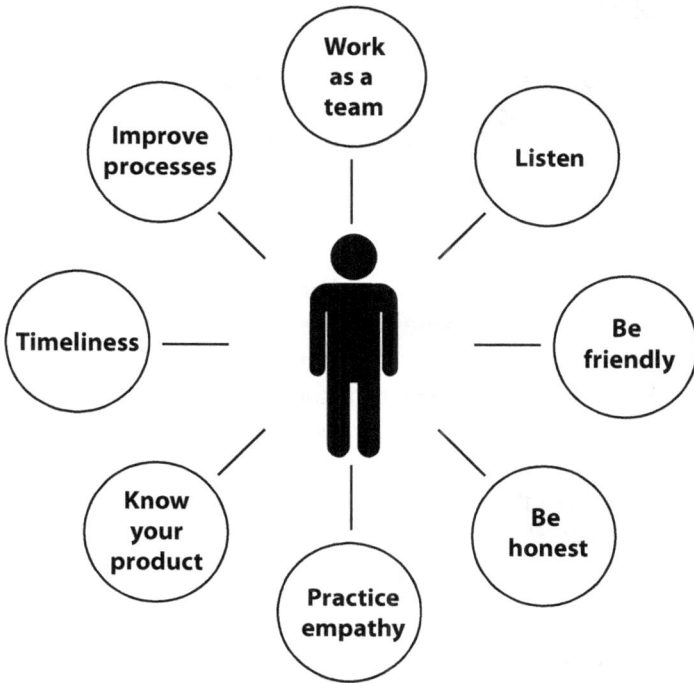

Customer service is an important aspect of your business operations. It attracts new customers and keeps current customers returning. By providing excellent customer service, your business can recoup its customer acquisition costs and cultivate a loyal following who will provide testimonials, reviews and referrals.

DEALING WITH CUSTOMER SERVICE CORRECTLY

I once answered the phone to a man screaming down the line about how I had poisoned his kids with the drinks served the previous night at my restaurant. He claimed they ordered five thick milkshakes with soy milk but were given regular milk. They were allergic to milk and had severe reactions. I asked him to come to the restaurant and I would happily refund him. While waiting, I asked my staff if they had remembered the order and what had happened, but they did not. I went through the sales receipts from the previous day to find the order to process the refund, but I could not find an order that matched with his complaint. When the man arrived, I asked him to complete an incident form with details of the time, date, any names, order details and complaint details. He became explosive, saying this was inappropriate and that his kids' lives were in danger. I said I needed the details to process a refund and would be unable to do so without them. I would also need a doctor's certificate linking the food poisoning to my store restaurant and products. He stormed out and didn't return.

After settling down, I realised it was a weird situation. My restaurant was based in a shopping centre, so I enquired at a few other cafés and asked if they'd had a similar situation. I discovered that four other businesses had had the same or a similar complaint. With this information, I went to the police and reported the situation. They retrieved the camera vision of the person, and I confirmed the suspect. A few months later, the police gave me an update. Apparently, these people had been running this scam through at multiple shopping centres, telling different versions of the story to cafés and supermarkets and had been getting away with thousands of dollars. They had finally been caught.

The moral of the story is to provide excellent customer service, but use your experience, knowledge, training, and instincts to make the best decision about a situation. It may not be the case that you have done the something wrong, but you will always need to deal with it correctly.

Loyalty

Your existing customers are your most predictable source of new revenue, as they already know and trust your business. Loyal customers, those who choose to return to your business, value their relationship with you over potential benefits that could be provided by one of your competitors.[20]

Your customers are not just worth the amount of money they spend in your business today; they have

20 S Bernazzani, 'Customer loyalty: The ultimate guide', Hubspot (24 January 2021), https://blog.hubspot.com/service/customer-loyalty, accessed 20 May 2021

future value if you can retain them. As such, you should bring customer loyalty into your marketing, strengthening your relationship through customer loyalty strategies. Selling to existing customers saves money. You will have better conversion rates from existing customers, who will continue to buy from you again and again unless they have a disappointing experience, so you need to be proactive in maintaining your relationship with them. You have already established trust and inspired confidence in your product – you may even know something about them, which makes it easier to identify their needs and predict their actions. You need to do less marketing to existing customers, meaning less time, effort and expense. It costs less to build a long-term relationship with an existing customer than to attract a new customer.

Focus on the customers who generate the most revenue and are likely to refer your business. One of the main reasons you want to promote a customer loyalty programme is to transition a loyal customer into a repeat customer. Loyalty programmes encourage your customers to return on a regular basis. Your regular and repeat customers are your most valuable customers. They may not make big purchases, but you need to look at the lifetime value of those purchases. Your customer lifetime value (CLV) metric is important and will tell you how well you are resonating with your customers.[21] You can

---

21 The Daily Egg, 'The importance of customer lifetime value (CLV) and how to calculate it' (3 December 2018), www.crazyegg.com/blog/customer-lifetime-value, accessed 20 May 2021

see how much your customers like your products and services and what you are doing right, as well as how you can improve. CLV is calculated as the average amount of money your customers have spent with your business over their entire purchase history, minus the amount of money you spent to acquire that customer.

REWARDING LOYAL CUSTOMERS

I used two different types of loyalty programme in my second restaurant. The first was a loyalty card where every tenth coffee was free; the second was my monthly newsletter. For signing up to the email database, I offered a free item with their next visit. This was an immensely popular strategy with more than 100 redemptions per month. The loyalty cards were more difficult to track because I would only receive them after thirty visits. When I developed Maralytics, I made sure that this type of campaign could be tracked and measured. Loyalty campaigns are great for rewarding your regular customers and keeping them coming back to your venue instead of going to the competition.

Referrals

A referral is when someone who has been to your business or experienced your service recommends you to a new customer. This may happen in conversation between friends, or you can create a formal referral marketing programme to encourage it.[22] Referrals are one of the most powerful selling and marketing tools available. A referral from a satisfied customer is the best source of new business and requires little to no effort. In the past, referrals came purely via word-of-mouth. Today, referrals rely more on social media and the internet, which gives the positive message a bigger reach and a broader audience.

Referrals can be formalised and incentivised within a referral programme. There are two types of referral programmes: non-incentive payment and incentive payment. Non-incentive payment referrals benefit the existing customer by providing a solution or giving them special treatment; incentive payment referrals are more popular and include rewards and formal agreements.

The most common non-incentive payment is word-of-mouth referrals. If you provide a great customer experience, a word-of-mouth referral will happen naturally. If you nurture and cultivate this, you will attract more customers. Word-of-mouth is dependent on loyalty, which you must earn. If you want your customers to rave about your business, you must please them. By going above and beyond for your customers, you give them a reason to talk about your business. The best word-of-mouth referrals come after you have provided the customer with exceptional value.

---

22 C Stec, '14 effective ways to get high-quality referrals from your customers', Hubspot (15 June 2020), https://blog.hubspot.com/service/how-to-get-referrals, accessed 20 May 2021

Enticing your customers to actively refer your business after they have had a positive experience is also great way to boost your brand image and increase customer trust by encouraging existing, happy customers to mention and share your brand. Offering incentives sweetens this experience. Whether it's a gift card, cash or a prize, give your customers something in return for connecting your business with warm leads – they deserve it. Without an incentive, you will rely on their generosity and ability to find time in their busy lives; adding a reward into the mix will get their attention.

ASKING FOR REFERRALS

While working in the training industry, I relied heavily on referrals. When working with a venue, I would qualify one or two staff members and then ask them for referrals. I could continue to work in the same place and use many of the same venue-specific documents for qualifications. I then had more time to spend assessing my trainees on their individual skills and strengths.

Summary

In this chapter, we looked at how unpacking sales can help you uncover more opportunities to take advantage of in your marketing strategies and convert potential customers to actual customers and sales. We looked at how the 4Ps of marketing can help you differentiate your business from your competition and stand out in your industry. Remember – you need to market the right product, in the right place, at the right price, in the right way.

We also learned about the sales cycle, a set of specific actions you can take to gain new customers and streamline your sales activity. This provides your business with reference points and shows you where in the cycle a customer is. A clearly defined cycle enables you to find potential customers, close the sale and retain those customers for repeat business and referrals in the future.

We found out that customer service is key to creating and retaining loyal customers, who are more profitable for your business. It is in your best interests to strengthen your relationships with these customers – they already know and trust your business and so are likely to refer you. This is important because satisfied customers are the best source of new business.

When sales and marketing work together, your business will see a substantial improvement in performance. Strong sales techniques are vital to driving business revenue and growth, but you won't have any customers if you lack an effective marketing plan. Striking a balance between sales and marketing requires a comprehensive strategy that smoothly guides leads and prospects toward becoming loyal customers that generate referrals.

9

Performance

When your business is performing, this means that everything is working smoothly and you are on a profitable trajectory. To improve your performance or increase growth, you need to build a plan, implement strategies and track the results to see when you have achieved your goals. By linking campaign objectives to their outcomes, you will know which strategies generate the best results and ROI and won't waste your marketing dollars on campaigns that do not perform.

Your marketing strategies should have KPIs attached to them to ensure you achieve the key objectives of your marketing plan. These provide clarification on the current position of your business and future performance expectations, creating predictability. The most important KPI is the impact a marketing campaign has on your revenue and profits. ROI is the simplest way to know if a campaign is profitable or not and can be used to compare campaigns using a base number or percentage. Generally, you want to make more than you spend on a marketing campaign.

Predictability, efficiency, effectiveness and reach all influence the performance of your marketing. Creating predictability in marketing is valuable. When marketing is predictable, it can drive sustainable growth by establishing exactly how much money needs be invested to generate a certain amount of revenue. Predictability allows you to forecast the future and create the goals and KPIs you need to keep your business viable and profitable. It gives you the ability to create a solid plan that you can scale effectively and use to improve customer loyalty and increase profits.

Efficiency and effectiveness will increase the performance of the campaigns in your marketing strategy. In theory, both lead to higher conversions and revenue. While the concepts differ, they have similar aims and rely on one another for optimal results. Finding the balance between these two measures in your marketing strategy can be a catalyst for tremendous growth.

Reach is another important performance metric for marketing campaigns. If you know the potential reach of a campaign, you can increase the potential ROI and create a more successful outcome. Knowing potential reach will help you determine whether the cost of a marketing campaign is worth the new customers it could attract and the impressions it could make.

There are many ways you can improve the performance of your marketing campaigns. The key to success lies in choosing the right campaigns, setting clear and attainable goals and reviewing your progress to ensure you are on the right track.

MARKETING CAMPAIGNS NEED TO BE PROFITABLE

If my marketing campaigns weren't profitable, they were discontinued. In my restaurants, I found that using supermarket vouchers (pre-social media) was hugely successful in attracting customers and sales. But after two years, I found that I was no longer increasing my sales/customers and the results had plateaued. I started experimenting with providing the same offer to the regular users of these vouchers, but directly from my website. After six months of transition, I stopped the supermarket vouchers and found that there was no change to my weekly sales revenue or customer count. Originally, it was a great campaign to attract new customers and keep them as regulars, but once I had exhausted that channel, it was time to try out new strategies.

KPIs

Your KPIs are quantifiable, outcome-based goals. Your marketing plan should include five to seven KPIs to keep track of your progress.[23] Understanding what is working and what is not working in your marketing is essential for your business operations and growth strategy. By tracking the right marketing KPIs you will be able to adjust your various marketing strategies and budgets.

All your marketing activities should be measurable. There is no excuse for not knowing your results. A good marketing KPI will demonstrate how effective your marketing strategies are in achieving the key objectives of your marketing plan.

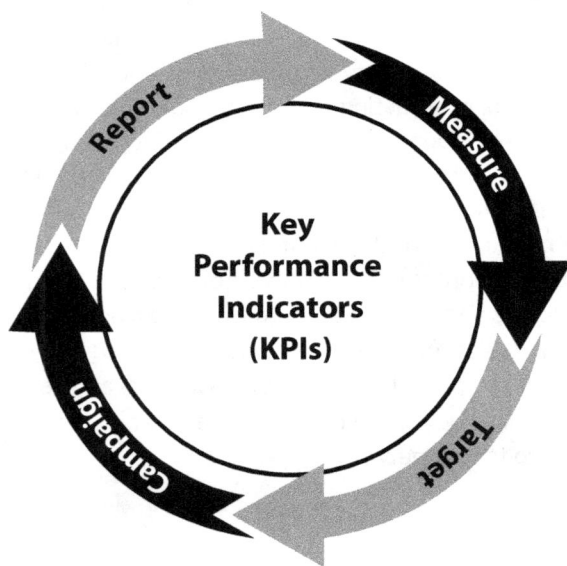

---

23 H Enochson, '27 examples of key performance indicators', OnStrategy (11 May 2021), https://onstrategyhq.com/resources/27-examples-of-key-performance-indicators, accessed 20 May 2021

There are four characteristics of a good marketing KPI:

1. **A measure:** A KPI must have a measure, the more detailed the better.

2. **A target:** A KPI needs to have a target, usually a numeric value that matches your measure and your goal.

3. **A campaign:** A KPI needs to be associated with a defined, trackable and measurable campaign.

4. **Reporting frequency:** If possible, report all your KPIs at the same time.

An example of a good KPI statement is: '5,000 leads from a one-month Facebook advertising campaign.' It has a measure (5,000), it has a target (leads), it has a campaign (Facebook advertising campaign) and it has a reporting frequency (one month). This statement meets all four elements of a good KPI.

Good KPIs provide clarity for your business. Use them for benchmarking and as a point of reference when making future or past comparisons. They keep you focused on the aspects that require your attention, are invaluable in the decision-making process and help to drive growth in your business. By using marketing KPIs you can see if you are moving forward or backward.

TRACKING KPIS AND MEASURING TARGETS

Every marketing campaign I implemented in my second restaurant had a KPI linked to it. Measuring the results and knowing if we had met our targets supported me with decision-making and forecasting in the business. The results were reported and measured monthly on spreadsheets to see if expectations had been met. I had one spreadsheet with five years of data for every marketing campaign I ran, its KPI and the results. I also created separate spreadsheets for each channel to measure their KPIs and results. Competitions were separate, as their KPIs and data were different from advertising and promotional campaigns.

Efficiency and effectiveness

Efficiency and effectiveness are two different but related measures of the success of your marketing strategy. They both theoretically lead to higher conversions and revenue and both have a similar aim. They are different but interdependent and can be a catalyst for tremendous growth.[24]

Efficiency measures the success of your processes. Measures of efficiency generally centre around minimising spend; in other words, where you see the same

---

24 A Soffer, 'Efficiency and effectiveness: the perfect marketing mix', Leadspace (20 August 2019), www.leadspace.com / efficiency-and-effectiveness-the-perfect-marketing-mix, accessed 20 May 2021

or better results at a lower cost. Typical measures of marketing efficiency include cost per acquisition (CPA), click through rates (CTR), conversion rates and visitor engagement activity. Identifying inefficiencies requires an honest evaluation of your marketing strategy. Look for where you are wasting time and eliminate these tasks or activities completely, or outsource to an automated platform or another team member.

Effectiveness measures the contributions that your marketing strategies make to the business. Are they generating revenue? How much? Typically, measures of marketing effectiveness are financial. They include revenue per visit, CLV and campaign ROI. Ineffectiveness is easy to spot. When you do not see the expected ROI from your marketing efforts, you need to identify the root cause so you can turn it around.

Do an audit of your marketing plan and strategy to see how you can increase the efficiency and effectiveness of your campaigns and performance. Look at where you can make your processes and systems more efficient. Are there bottlenecks and mistakes being made? An audit will highlight where an inefficiency could be holding you back. Look also at where you can improve your effectiveness. Can you change or tweak something to get a better result? Using either or both measures can make a big difference to the results you get from your marketing activities.

LOOKING AT WHAT YOUR MARKETING CAMPAIGN OFFERS

In the early days of marketing campaigns for my second the restaurant, I experimented with different call-to-actions. The results were measured to see which ones had the best ROI. There was one campaign I did using one channel with two different offers. This campaign was a supermarket voucher, and the channel was two competing supermarkets. The offer was a 20% discount off meals in the first supermarket and a 'buy one, get one free' through the alternative. The results were dramatically different. The discount voucher returned a result of twenty customers, and the 'buy one, get one free' had a result of 460 customers in the same month. By using these results, I could see the effectiveness of each (twenty redemptions compared to 460 redemptions), and the inefficiency of the offer between the two channels (20% discount compared to 'buy one, get one free').

Reach and impressions

The reach of a marketing campaign is the size of the potential audience. Related to this, the number of impressions tells you how many times your ad was actually shown to this audience. Reaching the right audience is critical to the success of your advertisements. To make the best marketing decisions, it is important to know how many people you will reach with your advertisements before they run. This will enable you to reach your desired audience with the most effective campaign plan. It does not tell you how many people will see your ad but it does tell you the potential audience, in other words the size of the opportunity to attract new customers.[25] Knowing how many customers you might reach allows you to make smarter decisions about where you spend your marketing dollars, minimising the risk of overspending on ineffective activities and helping you create the most profitable campaigns. If you know how many potential new customers you will reach, you can also make sure you have enough products available to sell, or sufficient capacity to serve these customers. When you have the numbers, you can use them strategically.

An impression is when an ad or content is shown to an audience. Impressions are counted each time your ad is shown on a search result page or at another site; they represent an opportunity for the ad to be seen, heard or influence a potential customer. The success of an impression marketing campaign may not always result in conversions, but tracking impressions can give you a better understanding to the visibility of your ad.

By knowing both the reach and impressions of an ad, you can determine whether the cost of a marketing campaign is worth the new customers it could attract. When you have the reach numbers, you can quantify how many impressions are needed to be

---

25 L Lake, 'Learn about market reach and why it's important', The Balance Small Business (19 September 2019), www.thebalancesmb. com/what-is-market-reach-2295559, accessed 20 May 2021

able to optimise your campaigns and create a good marketing mix.

FACEBOOK MARKETING

Facebook marketing is a great way to determine the reach of any ad campaigns you plan to run. When you nominate the target audience of your advertisement, Facebook tells you the potential reach results. This is amazing data. In the reports section after the campaign has finished, Facebook will tell you how many impressions the ad generated.

ROI

Return on investment, or ROI, is a key cost-related performance measure. ROI is a popular metric because it helps to determine marketing budget allocation and to identify activities in the marketing mix that should continue to be funded and those that should be cut. You should use your ROI metric to compare different campaigns or channels within your marketing strategy, prioritising and repeating the campaign with the largest ROI.

Digital footprint data is valuable in enabling you to see what your customers are looking at, but it is not related to your financial performance. Conversion data tells you exactly when and where a customer took an action. When you analyse your conversions, you will get a clearer picture of your results and performance, and what marketing activity is driving it.

ROI and related metrics provide a snapshot of profitability and what is driving it, which enables you to make planning decisions and forecasts based on the position of your efforts and the returns that you are expecting. ROI is a popular metric because of its versatility and simplicity. The calculation is not complicated and is easy to understand and use in a wide range of scenarios. To calculate the ROI, you calculate the value of a campaign divided by the cost. Depending on the scenario, you might measure the value as sales transactions or number of customers.

$$(Sales - Cost) \div Cost = ROI$$

The general goal is to make more than a dollar for every dollar you spend on a marketing campaign. If the ROI is positive, it is usually worthwhile continuing the campaign. If there are campaigns with higher ROI, prioritise these. On the flip side, if any campaigns have a negative ROI, withdraw them quickly to reduce their impact on the business performance.

Measuring ROI helps you to answer the most commonly asked question: is this campaign profitable? But marketing ROI and sales generated are not the only important numbers to focus on. Other metrics can also demonstrate the effectiveness of a marketing campaign. The type of metrics you want to track will vary for different marketing objectives. Business owners will want to see an overview for every marketing channel, while marketing managers will want to dive deeper to understand the day-to-day performance.

Some common metrics and results to measure are:

- Conversion rates
- Profit per campaign
- Lifetime value of a customer
- Customer acquisition costs
- Customer retention costs
- Campaign ROI
- Campaign profit
- Campaign sales

LOOKING AT YOUR ROI

I would always keep a competition or marketing campaign running if it was generating great results. When I would review and analyse the results of campaigns, I would compare the ROIs. For example, the first and the fifth competitions I ran at my second restaurant cost the same amount of money to produce, approximately $1,000, but the results were vastly different. The first competition generated 670 entries, $18,659 in sales and had an ROI of

17.17%. The second competition generated 1,012 entries, $32,034 in sales and had a ROI of 29.42% – an all-round winner.

Predictability

The ability to predict the future is a useful skill to have in business. Being predictable means doing the same thing in the same way, every time. When you have predictability in your marketing, you know how well your activities will do, can have confidence in what you are doing and avoid poor decisions in the future. When marketing becomes predictable, it can drive sustainable growth with the knowledge of exactly how much needs to be invested to generate a certain level of revenue.

Being unpredictable can damage trust in a business, causing misunderstandings and mistakes. People want to avoid stress and anxiety in their workplace and few things are more stressful than not knowing what is going to happen or being surprised by disappointing situations.

Predictability allows you to forecast the future and create goals and KPIs that will keep the business viable and profitable. It provides the ability to create a solid plan that can be effectively scaled to improve customer loyalty and increase profits. When your marketing results are predictable, you can rely on a regular cashflow, be able to budget each month and enjoy compound returns over time.

Campaign	Consistency	Customers	Channels
Campaigns need to attract customers with a good CTA	Produce and run campaigns regularly	Who, where and what your customers want	Focus on the media channels that will be the most effective

There are four ways to create marketing predictability:

1. **Campaign:** Your campaign needs to attract customers with a good CTA.

2. **Consistency:** You need to produce and run campaigns regularly.

3. **Customers:** You need to know who your customers are, where they are and what they want.

4. **Channels:** You need to focus on the media channels that will be the most effective.

By creating predictability, you will be rewarded with better results, happier staff and make a better impression on first-time customer experiences. Systems facilitate predictable outcomes. One of the main reasons a business loses customers is because it fails to deliver a consistent, predictable experience. This disappoints the customers and they go elsewhere. Predictability in the form of consistency has a positive psychological impact, both on the business and its customers.

You will feel more confident and prepared in your marketing campaigns and exude control, trust and reliability.

HAVING A STANDARD OFFER

My standard offer for all my promotional vouchers was 'buy one, get one free' coffee. The channel and campaign type were different, but the offer was the same. This offer became part of my brand strategy and customers knew that it ran continuously. If they wanted to redeem the offer, they just had to look for it. After testing other offers, I found this one always provided the most predictable results.

Summary

In this chapter, we looked at things that can measure and improve your marketing performance, including KPIs, efficiency, effectiveness, reach, impressions and predictability. Businesses need to run lean and improve their marketing activities to increase their performance; measuring your marketing is the best way to do this.

KPIs express what you want to achieve with your marketing plan; they should be linked to a campaign directly to measure its outcome. It's important to make your campaigns as efficient and effective as possible. By making your campaigns more efficient, you can have a better result at a lower cost; by making your campaigns more effective, you can generate more revenue.

Marketing reach is the number of potential customers who could see a specific campaign or advertising activity. When you know the potential reach, you can determine the number of impressions you want to show new customers. At the end of the campaign, you can review the marketing ROI to see if it was profitable or not. This is the easiest way to identify which campaigns you should continue to use in your marketing plan.

Once you have established that you have a good, effective and efficient campaign, you want to make it predictable. Predictability allows you to forecast and set goals to keep the business viable and profitable. Remember that marketing is the bridge between your business and your customers; you want to make sure your marketing will improve growth and lead to good performance.

PART FOUR

IDENTIFY

M arketing is a catalyst for growth – the more successfully you market, the more opportunity there is to grow your business. Identifying what in your marketing fosters growth is critical.

Your outcomes are the end game, they are where you want to get to via your marketing. To get clarity on your desired outcomes, in this part we'll break them down into smaller components. Your marketing vision or vision statement establishes the pathway to the outcomes. Goals set the direction for what your marketing needs to do. Objectives are the steps on the way to reaching your goals. Strategies dictate the activities by which you will achieve the marketing objectives. Campaigns are sets of activities in pursuit of a strategy; each campaign requires a clear purpose and identity.

Reports can show if your campaigns are fulfilling goals, generating sales and bringing in revenue. Without a marketing report, you are flying blind, so it is vital that reports and reporting become a core part of your marketing operations and workflows. All the information needs to be turned into digestible data so you can make sense of it.

Keeping track of daily weekly and monthly marketing results data means you will always have a visual overview of your data from a granular level to the bigger picture. The best way to optimise your marketing is to have the ability to toggle between the campaign metrics and the overall strategy, so you can make changes to increase performance and progress toward your goals. Data fragmentation is the single greatest barrier to creating and optimising a comprehensive, holistic marketing strategy. I developed Maralytics as a solution to aggregate all the data from every channel and provide reports that make it easier to make decisions – decisions about potential opportunities, planning and implementing campaigns, marketing performance and control.

Breaking everything down into smaller chunks gives a clearer picture on what you want to achieve and the difference you want to make with your business. This makes it much easier to spend your energy and funds more efficiently, meaning you can focus your marketing efforts in the most cost – and time-effective way.

10
Outcomes

Starting with a clear, concise and focused marketing vision establishes a pathway for you to follow and defines exactly what you are wanting to achieve. It is easier to adopt new marketing initiatives that move you closer to your vision, pivoting your focus to clearly reflect the desired outcomes or put in extra effort for a particular aspect of your brand that is working in service of your vision. Documenting your aspirations in a vision statement captures the essence of where you want your marketing to take you and inspires you to reach your goals.

Goals set the direction for what needs to happen within your marketing to create successful strategies and campaigns. You should define your goals in a way that clearly communicates what you want to accomplish and what you see as the criteria for success.

When you have clear marketing objectives, you can start prioritising the actions that will move you towards your goals. Marketing objectives are a pivotal part of a marketing strategy. They are actionable, specific and measurable targets designed to provide a focus on clear and specific actions. When you take the time to outline objectives and measure their impact, you can tell when your marketing efforts are having an impact.

Marketing strategies are the activities through which you will achieve the marketing objectives; they are the plan of action. When you create a strategy, you are ensuring that your activities are targeting the right people with relevant content that will appeal to them. The more time you spend creating clear strategies, the more opportunities you create to sell. Your marketing strategies should inform your marketing campaigns.

Marketing campaigns need to have an identity and a purpose, which should be consistent with your brand. They need to be consistent and focused with short-term activities intended to achieve a specific goal, to bring about a specific result, promote a product or service and reach customers in a variety of ways over multiple media platforms.

HAVING A PASSION FOR OWNING A BUSINESS

Owning a restaurant, I got to know many other business owners. I often saw them lose sight of the reason why they started their business. It is easy to get caught up in the daily operations, workload, the problems, customer/staff issues, paying bills, and being busy. For me, the reason to own a business is to have freedom, time, and money to support my lifestyle. When I have these outcomes in my daily life, I am fulfilled and have a passion for what I do.

Vision statement

Your vision statement is a vivid description about what you want your marketing to be, and where it is taking you, to inspire and motivate you. A well-defined vision creates a mental picture of what you are wanting to achieve. Being clear on your marketing vision involves knowing what you are working towards, so clearly define the problem and the solution. Your vision outlines your end goal.

Defining your marketing vision provides:

- Clarity

- Focus

- Milestones

- Purpose

- Expectations[26]

---

26 SJ Davidson, 'Define your marketing vision for clarity, focus and drive', StuartJDavidson.com (no date), http://stuartjdavidson.com/marketing-vision, accessed 20 May 2021

Vision is the heart of the business and should provide an outline for all your plans for change and aspirations for growth. It helps set the direction of the business and motivates employees to implement and execute your plans. Remember, marketing is a catalyst for growth – the more successfully you market, the more opportunity there is to grow your business.

Formalise your vision by writing down your marketing vision statement. Documenting your aspirations within a clear statement will capture the essence of where you want your marketing to take you, and inspires you and your team to reach your business goals. When you have this statement, it will guide every decision, choice and activity in your marketing department. A strong marketing vision statement will help to differentiate your marketing activities and make you stand out from competitors.

The common traits of a successful vision statement are as follows:

- **Concise:** It should be simple, easy to read and only include the essentials.

- **Clear:** The clearer the statement is, the easier it is to focus on and achieve.

- **Future-orientated:** Write it for where you plan to be, so you are striving toward it.

- **Stable:** It should not be affected by market or technological changes.

- **Inspiring:** Something that will rally the team and be desirable for everyone involved.

The vision is important to hold onto, especially on the most difficult days, and should serve as a reminder for you and your team of what your future goals and objectives are. Your vision statement is your overall marketing plan and purpose. It is your brand.

A SIMPLE VISION STATEMENT

My marketing vision statement for Maralytics is remarkably simple: 'Marketing must be transparent because business success relies on it.'

Marketing goals

Goals are an essential component of your marketing plan. They are your starting point because they set the direction for what needs to happen with your marketing to create successful strategies and campaigns. If you want to succeed, you need to set goals that you genuinely want to achieve. Without goals, you will lack focus and direction. Goals also provide a benchmark to measure your achievements and keep you aware of your progress.

Goal setting is a powerful process that helps you decide where you want to go with your marketing. You need to think about the future of your business and what motivates you and your team. By knowing precisely what you want to achieve, you know where you need to concentrate your efforts. You can easily spot the distractions or deviations that will prevent you from getting your desired results.

Marketing goals are the endpoints you want to reach with your marketing. They are different from your business goals, as they are what you are trying to achieve specifically with your marketing. They are a pivotal part of the overall marketing strategy and are the key to successful campaigns and advertising.

The purpose of marketing is to reach your target audience and communicate to them the benefits of your products and/or services, so you can attract customers.

Some examples of marketing goals are:

- Building or broadcasting brand awareness
- Generating leads
- Establishing leadership and credibility
- Revenue generation
- Increasing brand engagement[27]

Once you are clear about what you want to achieve with your marketing, create your goals. What matters most is defining goals that clearly communicate what you want to accomplish and what you see as the criteria for success.

SIMPLE GOALS

Goals are like visions. They are the future that you want to achieve. The goals that I had for the restaurants were to attract more customers and generate revenue. I always like to keep it nice and simple.

Marketing objectives

Marketing objectives are the steps on the way to achieving your goals and provide a clear direction.

---

27 Skyword, 'Marketing goals', Skyword (29 November 2016), www. skyword.com/marketing-dictionary/marketing-goals, accessed 20 May 2021

They are actionable targets designed to keep your focus on clear and specific actions, which should align with the marketing and business goals. Objectives outline how you plan to reach the goal and what impact that will have on the business. They are specific and measurable and are designed to provide both instruction and targets. Without defined objectives, your marketing goals will lack clarity and follow-through. When you do not take the time to outline objectives and measure their impact, you cannot tell if your marketing efforts have had any impact. Marketing objectives should follow the SMART philosophy to be effective; this means they need to be **S**pecific, **M**easurable, **A**ttainable, **R**elevant and **T**ime-based. When you use this technique to create your objectives, you set a finish line for your marketing team to move towards and add a level of accountability.

The first step in creating a useful list of marketing objectives is to review your goals, as your objectives should be aligned with them. Some examples of marketing objectives are:

- To increase blog subscribers by 25% month on month

- To increase Facebook likes and followers to 10,000 in six months

- To get sixty positive five-star Google My Business reviews in three months

- To increase the average customer spend by 50% in three months

As you can see from these examples, you need to know what you are aiming for and by when to know whether you are on track to achieve it.

HAVING CLEAR OBJECTIVES

For a long time, I was confused by the difference between goals and objectives – and it seems other people are too. Goals provide the overall context of what you want to achieve. Objectives describe the exact result you want to deliver. Having clear objectives makes them easier to achieve. When you do not have objectives, it is easy to waste money, promote randomly and have lots of highs and lows. With clear objectives, you know exactly what the target is and how to get there.

Marketing strategies

Marketing strategies are the activities and components you employ to achieve your marketing objectives. They are your plan of action. Results do not happen by chance. The more time you spend building clear strategies made up of multiple complementary activities, the more opportunities you create to sell and move closer to your objectives.

Strategies encompass the bigger picture and provide you with a template to inform your campaigns. They create a sense of stability and predictability within the marketing department. A marketing strategy is like a café menu. It is a repeatable process and framework. It may change or have items added, but at the core it remains the same. The goal of the menu is to provide food to customers. The objectives are, for example, brand awareness or lead generation, which correspond to the sections of the menu, like breakfast, lunch and dinner. The strategies are the dishes within each of these sections; they include different ingredients (different types of marketing activities) like digital marketing, social media, offline marketing, email marketing, SEO, PPC, video marketing and so on. While the recipes (campaigns) are adaptable and can be altered, the menu and dishes (strategies) generally stay the same. This allows you to spend more time improving your recipes and perfecting the dishes, rather than changing the menu.

CONNECTING YOUR MARKETING GOALS WITH YOUR VALUES

My goal in marketing the restaurants was to attract more customers. My objective was to increase sales by 15% in one month, and the strategy I used was an RSPCA fundraiser. This strategy ran for six weeks and was a special event that I could implement easily as it did not disrupt normal operations. The fundraiser created a connection with the community and my values, while raising funds and awareness for the charity.

Marketing campaigns

Marketing campaigns are focused, short-term activities designed to bring about a particular result. They promote a specific project, product or service through different types of media, but are more than just advertising and also set out the logistics of a specific project. They typically aim to reach customers in a variety of ways and can be implemented over multiple media platforms.

Promoting a campaign is a straightforward process. When planning your campaign, you need to consider what you want your customers to do when they see, read or hear it. Having a clear campaign goal and purpose in line with your overall marketing goals and strategy is key to creating the most effective campaigns. It is wise to measure your campaign results to see if your marketing efforts are taking you closer to your goals and driving overall performance.

Your marketing campaign needs to have an identity, which is both an extension of your business' brand and a brand in itself. A big part of this is the campaign assets, which you can create yourself, use an agency or have the relevant media platform do for you.

Your choice of media platform(s) will depend on your target customers' preferences, locations, budget and engagement levels, so stick to the channels you already know you have success with. Marketing campaigns usually run over a set period with a defined start and end date and should drive a desired action or result via a clear call-to-action, directly asking your customers to do something that will benefit them.

MULTIPLE CAMPAIGNS WITHIN ONE STRATEGY

I ran multiple campaigns within my RSPCA strategy, including a fundraiser merchandise box, sponsorship for my staff doing the Million Paws Walk and a special vegan menu.

The merchandise box was ordered from the charity; we raised funds and awareness for the charity by selling products from the box. From a logistics perspective, procedures needed to be created for merchandise stocktake and financial reconciliations. The Million Paws Walk sponsorship collected money from customers and staff members to support those who were walking with their pets in the event. The vegan specials were created by the chef and we promoted them on the specials board and social media platforms.

I also ran additional campaigns on social media platforms, promoting our RSPCA fundraising strategy. This involved daily posts with photos of the food specials, merchandise items or any other special content. In the newsletter I sent to my database, I included special discount offers and promoted the month-long campaign.

Summary

In this chapter, we broke down the different outcomes of your marketing plan, including your vision, goals, objectives, strategies and campaigns. With clarity on each component, you will achieve more specific results that move you in a forward direction.

Your marketing vision statement outlines how you plan to change and improve your business. This serves as a reminder for you and your team of the direction in which you are heading.

Marketing goals are the endpoints that you want your marketing to get you to. To succeed, you need to set goals. Marketing objectives are a specific outline of how your goals will be achieved; they are the steps on the way that take you in the right direction. They tell you how you will reach the goal and what impact it will have on the business.

Your marketing strategies ensure you are targeting the right people with relevant content that will appeal to them, creating more opportunities to sell. With your marketing strategies, you will run campaigns. These have consistent themes and specific goals and use different media and channels to promote a particular product or service to the target audience. They have a set start and finish date, and you need to have clear campaign goals in mind before you start.

A successful marketing plan will be built around and deliver all these outcomes, which individually and collectively impact your results.

11
Data

Keeping track of daily, weekly and monthly marketing data ensures that you have a granular level as well as bigger picture view of what's going on in the business. To optimise your marketing, you need to toggle between the campaign metrics and the overall strategy, so you can make changes to increase performance and move closer to your goals.

Your metrics tell a story and show you a detailed picture of your marketing efforts. Marketing metrics measure the effectiveness of campaigns across all marketing channels, determining if it is successful or not. Surveys are a way of collecting these metrics and other qualitative information that can give you that detailed picture. Once you have collected all the data and metrics you need, you can use tools or platforms to visualise and analyse it so you can then go on to review your campaign results and make decisions. One particularly helpful way to have constant overview of the headline data in real-time is a dashboard, where you can easily check on performance results and get a high-level overview of what's going on with your marketing efforts without having to delve into detailed statistics.

TRACKING YOUR SALES RESULTS

All your data is trackable on the internet. In my last two restaurants, I wanted to know the financial and customer acquisition data for every marketing campaign. I had been collecting this information manually for many years as I had not found any program that could do this. This is why I created Maralytics. The software can connect a customer transaction to a marketing campaign and import this information to the platform so you can create a report. This allowed me to see what my campaigns were achieving and focus on what I was most interested in – in my case, this wasn't how many impressions one of my social media posts got, but the actual sales generated.

Metrics

Marketing metrics measure the effectiveness of your campaigns. The metrics that you monitor will depend on what type of campaign you are running and what channels you have chosen to use. There are many different types of metrics you can measure and different platforms and technology will use different ones, which can be confusing.

Vanity metrics are the most commonly found and the easiest to measure. Examples of these include likes, follows, connections, engagement and shares. An increase in these numbers is good but does not necessarily indicate an increase in revenue, so make sure they are not the only metrics you use to measure the effectiveness of your campaign.

Digital footprint metrics are more useful. They enable you to track a user's online journey and use this information to engage your customer at different points in the sales cycle or remarket to them. Google Analytics is a free tool that can help you gather this data. Examples of digital footprint metrics include impressions, CTR, bounce rates, conversion rates, cost per click (CPC), opt-in rates, open rates, response rates, time on page and page scroll depth. This may seem like a lot of metrics (depending on your campaign) but keeping an eye on these numbers will give you an accurate assessment of your campaign and where you can improve it.

Performance metrics are the sales, revenue, profit and customer acquisition results. Alongside your campaign data, this provides unique insights into how your customers are behaving, which marketing channels are driving performance and how well budget is being spent. This tells you exactly how to (or how to not) run your next campaign.

Your metrics provide you with a detailed picture to better understand your marketing activities and efforts. Choosing the right marketing metrics for your business can be difficult and will be dependent on your industry and specific marketing goals.

CAMPAIGN METRICS

Every component of the RSPCA fundraising strategy I ran was measured. I counted the sales from merchandise and the donations that were collected. I documented the specials that were sold and compared the most popular special menu items. Redeemed social media vouchers and the newsletter special offers were tracked, measured and reported. This information was collated so the metrics could be imported into the report and I could see how successful the strategy was, and how it compared to the other fundraisers I ran.

Analytics

Analytics are measures of marketing performance that can help to maximise the effectiveness of your marketing activities, campaigns and optimise your ROI. Using analytics allows you to monitor campaigns and their outcomes, helping you to re-evaluate your marketing spend and avoid wasting money.[28] They also offer insights into your customers' preferences and current trends.

Using analytics to see how marketing drives revenue helps to demonstrate a campaign's value and justify its cost. By making the invisible visible through metrics and insights, it is easier to accurately assess and prove campaign performance instead of relying on guesswork and assumptions. Having this level of insight gives you a deeper understanding of the impact of your marketing on revenue. You can set more realistic targets, gauge progress towards your goals and adjust on the fly, if necessary, to hit targets and KPIs.

A data-driven campaign requires the ability to quickly identify what is working and what isn't, the flexibility to respond to evolving marketplaces and the capacity to demonstrate value to the management team. To this end, robust analytics are a must and you should seek out a platform that provides visibility of accurate campaign ROI. These insights mean you can allocate spend more effectively across top-performing channels, ultimately boosting your results. There are many programs that can provide reports for activity on their own platforms, such as Google Analytics and Facebook Analytics. They look at their own digital

---

28 WordStream, 'Marketing analytics – success through analysis' (no date), www.wordstream.com/marketing-analytics, accessed 20 May 2021

footprint results, which includes any online activity, advertising results and measured engagement.

FINANCIAL ANALYTICS

When I was researching analytics programs, I could not find any software or program that could track financial or acquisition results. This surprised me. There are heaps of analytics apps available, but these all collect data from your digital footprint. Everything you do online leaves a mark, so I naturally assumed that there was a program that could track the financial returns on marketing activities. There wasn't. I wanted a solution to this problem and when I talked to other business owners, they wanted it too – this is how Maralytics started. I developed it to be able to tell me how much money a campaign generates, how much customers spend, or what the profit is for an individual campaign or activity across any type of campaign or channel.

Survey data

The purpose of a survey is to collect specific information from a particular group of people. Surveys are a great way to get feedback, as they enable you to collect qualitative rather than numeric data (ie metrics and KPIs) about how your business is performing. This is the most effective way to gather information on why individuals are or are not taking a particular action, which you can use for your business.

Online surveys are the most common type of survey that are used. Online platforms like Google Forms and Survey Monkey are automated tools for creating a survey, with lots of templates and recommended questions that you can ask your customers, clients or target audience.

When you design a survey, for it to be successful you should:

- Know your goal or purpose

- Identify your audience

- Have clear questions

- Do a pre-test to make sure it works the way you designed it

- Distribute it via the right channels

When you do all of this and get the survey out to a large group of people, you can collect some valuable data and a variety of responses. The more responses you get, the clearer the results will be.

Surveys are a great way to collect qualitative consumer data, get honest feedback and (hopefully) validation from your customers and find out if you are meeting the expectations of your business. The insights they generate can be used to make decisions and suggest changes. Surveys give your customers and prospects a voice and uncover their 'why'.

CUSTOMER VALIDATION

Every year in my second restaurant, I would update the menu and increase the prices. For several weeks prior to this, I would use my specials board to test how my customers would respond to new menu items that I wanted to introduce. I directed my staff to ask the customers who had ordered a special if they thought it was a good item to add to our new menu and we would record their responses. In the monthly newsletter and at the counter, I would have a survey request form for customers to complete, so I could find out what items they wanted added to the menu. By utilising several methods of collecting customer feedback, my job of creating a new menu was made much easier, as the customers had already told me what they wanted.

Visualising data

Data is normally numerical, which can be hard to get your head around. Translating numbers into graphs, charts and images provides a visual representation of your key metrics so that you can understand the data and what it is telling you quickly. In marketing, most of your decisions are based on patterns and trends. Visualising your data helps those patterns and trends to stand out, so that you can explore the topic further and uncover why those trends are emerging and what's driving certain results. You can then adjust your strategy and tactics accordingly.

Your brain processes visuals in a different way to numbers, and it is easier for your brain to understand messages that are conveyed through images.[29] Charts and graphs are useful for expressing complex data in a simple visual format. They also add value to your reports (discussed in the next chapter) by improving the clarity and effectiveness of the message that your data is telling you. When creating graphics, be mindful of what type of information you want to present. Do you want to highlight a trend (in which case a graph plotting results over time may be best), or do you want to show, for example, the percentage of sales coming from different sources (pie charts are great for this)?

Once you have identified the data you want to present visually, you need to decide which is the best tool to use for this. You can start with an Excel spreadsheet, or you can look online for a platform that creates various charts you can use to display your data. Remember, you will only get valuable insights from good quality, relevant data. Messy data leads only to assumptions and guesswork and will not give you a framework to optimise your marketing campaigns. If you want to compare channels or look at the overall results from your marketing mix, use a platform where you can aggregate the results from all your campaigns and channels. Finally, if the data does not support your

29 The Mind Tools Content Team, 'Charts and graphs', Mind Tools (no date), www.mindtools.com/pages/article/, accessed 20 May 2021

point of view, do not manipulate it or skew it to make it look like it does. This is this unethical, unhelpful and is also easy for an experienced data analyst to spot.

GRAPHICALLY REPRESENTING YOUR DATA

In my second restaurant, I would make decisions based on the data I collected in Excel. When I was testing Maralytics, I uploaded this same data to the program and was surprised to see a different perspective on those same numbers. I had a new awareness of how the campaigns looked compared to how I saw them in the past when they were just numbers on a spreadsheet. Having visual graphs and charts made understanding what the numbers meant much easier and I got different insights.

Dashboards

One incredibly helpful and visual form of data reporting is dashboards, which give you a real-time overview of your marketing data. The information dashboards provide at a glance can help you make quick and/or urgent marketing decisions, if you spot that something is performing particularly well/badly.

A marketing dashboard answers the question: how are your marketing efforts performing right now? Using your marketing dashboard means you do not have to run a full marketing report every time you want to check on an ongoing objective, you can quickly view the headline results as they are happening.

Dashboards monitor ongoing work and progress to help inform decision-making and marketing spend. They present your marketing metrics in an easy to read and visual way that keeps everyone aware of performance and up to date with real-time knowledge. With this type of visibility, you can correct any campaign issues at soon as they arise rather than waiting for these to become evident in monthly or quarterly reports. For example, by monitoring the performance of a digital advertising campaign on Facebook in real time, you can spot problems early and make changes before the costs add up. If you wait until the end of the campaign or even the end of month, the costs of mistakes can be significant and affect the campaign ROI.

USING DASHBOARD TO VIEW MARKETING ACTIVITIES

I developed the Maralytics program dashboard so I can see all my campaign results for any marketing activity. It is easy to display the results I want to view, and I can make fast decisions with a quick look at the dashboard.

Putting in time and effort to compile a marketing report just to get an update on progress is like scheduling a formal meeting to simply to check in with your team's progress. Who needs to waste time in a thirty-minute meeting when updates can be shared in a quick email? Your marketing dashboard is your quick email update on marketing progress.

Summary

In this chapter, we looked at how in every business you should track, measure and review your data so you can grow your revenue. You need to recognise and report the results of your marketing campaigns using metrics to determine the overall success of your activities.

Marketing metrics show the effectiveness of the campaign. Surveys capture qualitative feedback and opinions from your customers, uncovering what is happening but also, crucially, why.

Bringing your data to life by presenting it visually makes patterns and trends clearer. It is easier to understand images and viewing information this way can shed new light on your data. Dashboards are a visual reporting tool that show you how you are performing right now. If you want to quickly access real-time information without having to run a full report, dashboards are the answer.

12
Reporting

Marketing reports provide you with a benchmark for how things are progressing, which channels and activities are working and which are not. While dashboards give you a helpful real-time overview of what's going on, reports go into more depth about where you should be focusing your marketing efforts, budget and time and so need to be at the centre of your marketing operations and workflows. Detailed reports can be created in various forms, depending on what information you want and need to monitor and analyse.

A marketing report is a collection of data from different marketing sources. It can turn a huge volume of data into digestible information that you can easily make sense of. Reports should be able to be understood by anyone involved in the business' decision-making processes. They provide a snapshot of your business activities in a particular area, in this case marketing, to evaluate the performance of a specific marketing campaign or effort. Good marketing reports give you all the data that you need to make a decision, take an action, justify your efforts and highlight your successes. These reports need detail so that they can identify trends, pulling out even the smallest patterns to explain how they contribute to your marketing campaign returns.

Management reports do not need to be as detailed but provide an overview of the business' performance and a holistic view of your marketing so that this information can be used strategically. In business, you need to make strategic and tactical decisions all the time – in identifying and setting goals, objectives and strategies for your marketing activities, about potential opportunities, and for planning and implementing campaigns. Marketing and management reports help you to make these decisions.

SURPRISING RESULTS

After the first beta launch of Maralytics, I created a report to see what the results were and if the objectives had been achieved. I found the results surprising, as it identified a new target audience. The software was designed for small to medium-sized businesses, especially in the hospitality, retail, tourism, entertainment, eCommerce and services, but when I analysed the report, I found 80% of the beta testers were marketers. Marketing was their core business and the software provided reports that validated the results of their efforts. Originally, I had not targeted or expected this market, but after reviewing the report, it made perfect sense.

Marketing reports

Marketing reports help improve communication, productivity, accuracy and timeliness by providing a critical analysis of each campaign and channel. They give you the opportunity to investigate any identified issues in depth to come up with a solution. Detailed reports also tell you what success you are having in specific areas of your marketing activities.

To identify success, you first need to define it. Setting the right objectives and KPIs is a good start, tracking and collecting the results is the next step. By creating a detailed report, you will get insights on outcomes of campaigns and whether they are aligned to the intentions, which will tell you what type of campaigns to plan for the future.

A report should have a purpose so that you can be clear on what it is telling you and recommending that you do based on the data and evidence it presents. All reports need to include an executive summary, goals, dates, objectives, key performance indicators, strategy, insights, variances / anomalies and outcomes, with supporting information. You should create a reporting system rather than producing them ad hoc, so that you have a repeatable process that can be used consistently and to compare activities.

A reporting process is highly valuable process if crafted properly. Reports need to be easy to read and understand and should be designed to incorporate your branding and colours. Packaging is important in marketing and performance reports are no exception.

To create great reports:

- Add section headers to make your report clearer and readable

- Include comments and notes to add your insights

- Incorporate images

- Section or split your marketing report according to your needs

- Customise with your own design

A report makes sense of all the information and data you have collected and turns it into insight. Slicing, dicing and analysing the data and connecting the dots between your marketing activities and goals helps you draw conclusions and lessons from your campaigns and strategies. It helps you to spot problems before they grow, as well as opportunities to increase and replicate success. The secret to a good marketing report is to keep it simple and use the information to tell a story.

Used well, marketing reports will:

- Enable you to consolidate marketing information from multiple sources

- Offer insights about customer behaviour and activity within the business and all marketing channels

- Help you better understand your marketing activities and improve future performance

- Help to achieve your business goals and optimise your activities

MARKETING REPORTS STREAMLINE YOUR PROCESS

In my second restaurant, I implemented many competitions over the years and perfected the strategy with each one. This was only possible by creating a report and using the historical information for comparisons. All the information about the competitions, results, opportunities and mistakes was documented and the reports verified my campaign successes.

I had three main objectives:

1. Increase customer spend
2. Celebrate an event
3. Partner with a local tourism operator

The objectives were always met. The KPI targets created matched my previous events, so it was easy to measure performance. Every competition became increasingly streamlined with improved performance results.

Types of reports

There are numerous types of marketing reports you can create depending on what information you want and need to monitor and analyse. Reports should be run on a regular basis, but sometimes you may have a one-off campaign and will need a report to review the results. Consider who is going to read your report and be sure that you include and present information that is relevant and that they will understand. Types of marketing reports that can be produced are:

- A marketing performance report

- A specific campaign report

- A marketing management report

- A blog traffic and leads report

- A website traffic and leads per channel report

- An online advertising performance report

- A social media engagement report

You can run a broad-scope report related to a marketing objective or one as detailed as a breakdown of individual campaign analytics. A campaign report will give you a picture of how different elements of a campaign performed in the context of the campaign objective; this type of report should go into detail about how each element of the campaign performed and review the specifics of each activity. A report based on a marketing objective could be focused on brand recognition, for example. In this type of report, you could include sales, sales per customer, cost per sale, ROI, CPC, budget, cost, conversion, cost per conversion, conversion rate, CTR, clicks, likes, followers, impressions, engagement rate and more. You can also create reports for specific types of data, such as a sales report or a social media report covering all the different channels you use, like Facebook, Twitter and LinkedIn. Below are some more examples of the types of reports you could run:

- **SEO reports** are relevant to many of the KPIs you need to be tracking like organic traffic, conversion rate, CTR, keyword ranking and link building statistics. With SEO reports, you can drill down further down to pinpoint how much of your traffic is coming from organic searches, with data like organic search visits, bounce rate, average page load time and pages per visit from organic searches.

- **Keyword reports** show which keywords bring you the most qualified organic traffic by tracking metrics like best-performing keyword by clicks, impressions, CTR and average position.

- **Social media reports** track your social media performance, optimise your social media campaigns and show your results for specific channels with KPIs for each, such as page likes, new likes, followers, follower growth, impressions, reach, frequency, engagement, shares, comments, clicks and video views.

- **PPC advertising reports** give you data on your clicks, including CPC, CPA, quality score, average position and CTR.

- **ROI reports** track your results from campaigns and can be used in conjunction with your marketing planning and budget. ROI reports include sales revenue, sales per customer, cost per customer, average sale per customer, sales per channel, sales per CTA, customers per channel, customers per CTA and ROI per campaign.

Using different types of marketing reports is essential, as each is a snapshot of your marketing activities that tells you whether a specific effort is performing. You can drill down further into your data and tweak the individual components of a campaign to create different outcomes. A marketing report presents the results of your marketing efforts and highlights the successes. Good marketing reports give you all the data that you need to decide and act; this is usually less than the total amount of data that you have.

TRACKING YOUR SALES RESULTS

All your data is trackable on the internet. In my last two restaurants, I wanted to know the financial and customer acquisition data for every marketing campaign. I had been collecting this information manually for many years as I had not found any program that could do this. This is why I created Maralytics. This software can connect a customer transaction to a marketing campaign and import this information to the platform so you can create a report. This allowed me to see what my campaigns were achieving and focus on what I was most interested in – in my case, this wasn't how many impressions one of my social media posts got, but the actual sales generated.

Management reporting

Management reporting is the collection and analysis of data specifically to make business decisions. These reports offer a high-level overview of your marketing performance so that information can be used strategically, and do not need to be highly detailed. A marketing management team is generally not interested in the details; they want to know the results of successful campaigns and, if any need to be cancelled, why and where the budget should be redirected.

KEEPING YOUR TEAM AWARE OF MARKETING ACTIVITIES

With my marketing activities, I only reported on ones that were relevant to the meeting agenda or had something that needed to be discussed. My management team were not interested in the details; they wanted to know the results of successful campaigns, and if any were cancelled, why and when would it happen.

Management reports provide insights that enable you to drive performance. By assessing changing expectations, identifying challenges and forecasting trends, you can present the data relevant to the goals and objectives that were created for your marketing activities. Connecting the information in the report to your business goals will show what is driving – or hindering – the marketing performance.

Management reports play a significant role in decision-making and fill important knowledge gaps in the reporting structure with detailed, real-time insights into all areas of marketing so that you can:

- Clearly identify areas that need improving to maximise ROI

- Flag any anomalies

- Make accurate forecasting predictions
- Make well-informed decisions about the future directions of your marketing activities, based on accurate and up-to-date data

Summary

In this chapter, we looked at how reporting helps you to create and maintain a successful marketing strategy and mix for your business. Reports help you and your management team to track results, identify patterns and trends and make decisions or come to an important conclusion – like which CTA to use, how many channels to promote your campaign on or how much money to spend on social media advertising. Reports are key to creating great strategies.

There are many types of marketing reports that you can create, depending on what information you're particularly interested in, for example a report on a particular marketing objective, an individual campaign, or management report with a high-level overview of your marketing efforts. Reports of all kinds play a significant role in guiding decision-making and presenting information in a digestible format so that everyone can benefit from the insights they provide.

PART FIVE

INNOVATE

As a marketer, you always need to be on the lookout for the latest and emerging trends. Innovation in marketing can mean finding new markets, creatively addressing customers' needs, creating new products, opening new promotional channels and setting new and improved KPIs and objectives. Your aim is to increase revenue opportunities, eliminate failing campaigns and spend marketing dollars wisely.

Applying analytics across marketing channels, campaigns and activities tells you how your marketing programmes are performing, enabling you to fine-tune and/or innovate your efforts, leading to greater revenue and profitability. Attribution is an analysis technique that looks at the customer journey and identifies the touchpoints for customer conversion. Split testing is another helpful technique to apply to your campaigns, to identify which activities produce the highest conversion results. Once you know which campaign is the most effective in converting prospective to actual customers, you'll want to repeat this activity. You can do this analysis on your existing campaigns using testing techniques, or you can emulate another business' proven concept.

For inspiration, look to your competitors to see if any of their methods may resonate with you or your customers. They may be using new or different technologies, or be adding a new spin on old ideas. Either way, you might be able to integrate their ideas into your own business. New technology and platforms encourage innovation in your marketing; if you adapt your content, you too can become a market leader in your industry.

Marketing forecasting will enable you to explore long-term projections for future trends, activities and targets for your business. Creating a forecast will help you move towards and achieve the vision for your business. This is accomplished by reviewing historical data and customer feedback, alongside qualitative and quantitative forecasting techniques.

As a business owner, seek innovation in your marketing activities while continuing to use your known and trusted methods, adapting them as necessary. By using your own data, you can uncover the best solutions and strategies for your business and that can be adopted and adapted within your marketing plan to create a winning formula.

13

Analysis

As a business owner, you need to know what progress you have made and the results your marketing has achieved so you can assess progress toward your goals. This is done through analysis of all your metrics to see if their direction is aligned to your goal or vision for the company. In this chapter, we will look at several ways that you can analyse and use the results presented in your metrics, dashboard and reports, to put this information into the context of your broader goals and vision as you look to the business' future.

A CLEAR VIEW OF THE DATA

At the end of every month, I would collate all the results from every marketing campaign that had been active, and add them to a main spreadsheet, and to their individual channel spreadsheets. This way I could view the data that I needed to make decisions about. I was able to see that the figures were in the correct ranges.

When I uploaded the data to Maralytics software, I got a very different view of the data as it was all visual in the dashboard. This allowed me to look at the data differently. I got a clear picture of how successful a lot of the campaigns were in comparison to other campaigns.

Analysing your marketing necessarily involves a focus on your data, as well as external and internal factors, and takes into consideration the strengths and weaknesses of the business. Through analysis, you will gain insights into your marketing activities, see how much room there is for improvement, what the market is doing and how aligned your current activities are with your bigger goals and objectives. The insights you gain from analysis of your marketing reports, combined with a wider market awareness, tell you the whole story of your marketing. From this, you can create and identify new opportunities to drive more revenue and customers to your business.

The purpose of marketing is to create more revenue for the business. You want to attract more customers to spend more money. Marketing analysis helps you to understand your customers better by finding out what they want so that you can provide them with whatever that is. When you gather the results, analyse the data and generate insights, so you can create new strategies and improve performance.

Post-campaign analysis

When a campaign comes to an end, the final step is to do a post-campaign analysis report. Your aim here is to understand how the different elements of your campaign performed in relation to the overall campaign objective, plus your wider objectives and KPIs.

The main advantages of post-campaign analysis are to:

- Understand what elements of the campaign worked well/not so well

- Learn how the target audience responded to the campaign

- Review the overall effectiveness of the campaign in service of the objectives

- Discuss the campaign results with key stakeholders

- Provide valuable learnings for future campaigns

You should be as clear as possible about the purpose of the campaign when you design it, so that at the end you can review how it measured up and where it is possible to make better decisions and improve the performance of campaigns in the future.

Here are some examples of questions to ask when reviewing campaigns:

- How could you have saved money?

- What could have been done differently?

- What did you learn from the campaign?

- How can you improve a campaign, audience, or marketing channel?

ANALYSING THE SUCCESS OF YOUR CAMPAIGNS

In my second restaurant, I collected the results of every marketing campaign for analysis. One of my most expensive campaigns was via a supermarket docket promotion. This campaign was active for two years and always generated between $3,000 to $4,500 per month, it only fluctuated with seasonality. On reviewing my marketing mix, I decided to cancel the campaign as I wanted to see if it would have a big impact on sales. I hoped to transition these customers to my website so they could continue utilising the offer. After three months, I analysed my sales and found that cancelling the campaign had not impacted my revenue or customer count. The campaign had fulfilled its purpose of attracting new customers to the business. When I could see that it was no longer providing additional value, I had the opportunity to explore other channels.

Insights

Once you have created a post-campaign report of your results and you've analysed what it's telling you, the last and most important step is to pull out the key insights regarding your performance. An insight is the discovery of a relevant, actionable and previously unrealised opportunity. Insights start as information, are filtered by analysis and then are acted on. Your insights become your 'why', providing a direction for your future marketing efforts.

Your ability to drive growth in your business is dependent on how you analyse your results and data to generate insights and then your ability to translate these insights into effective action. Using your insights, you can focus on the bigger picture of improving your marketing activities to attract more customers, increase sales revenue and enable better forecasting of future activities. You will know where to spend time, money and effort, which will improve your cashflow and business performance.

Insights help your business spark innovation, uncover promising sources of growth and develop or maintain successful products and services. By applying the insights derived from your data, you can develop innovative and differentiated marketing strategies to apply in your marketing plan. Planning is important for creating the pathway and milestones; results tell you what happened; and insights help you to optimise and strategise.

LEARNING WHAT WORKS FOR YOUR BUSINESS

By reporting and analysing the results from all my marketing activities in the restaurants and generating insights, I could see what worked and what did not and could eliminate campaigns that were wasting money. It was also great to have data to show advertising sales reps, as they liked to see results.

At one time, I advertised in a seniors' publication because I'd noted that most of my regular customers were elderly. After three months of paying for advertising space, the results I collected were disappointing. I had assumed by promoting to the demographic of my customers, this channel and type of campaign would work well, but it did not.

You cannot assume you know which campaigns will bring in expected results. To find out for sure try everything you can and measure the results. You cannot instinctively know what message is reaching your customers and bringing them into your business to spend money. When you have tracked, reported and measured different campaigns and channels, then analysed the results, you will have the insights that tell you for sure what works best for your business.

Improvements

Generally, you will analyse your campaign performance once it is complete, once you have collected and reported your results. However, there are ways you can optimise your campaign results while they're in progress and dramatically improve them. For example:

- Increase the duration or give more time to sell a campaign will drive better results. If you can improve the efficiency, you should be able to increase the revenue with little or no investment or effort.

- Streamline productivity, so you can focus on sales that will generate more revenue.

- Improve conversion rates by closing any leaks in each step of your pipeline.

- Recycle and re-engage your prospects or customers to keep them in your sales cycle.

- Identify the best-performing marketing campaign and copy it across other channels.

- Add more customers to the pipeline by increasing the number of campaigns you have active.

- Review your workplace processes and resources and improve efficiency to speed up the sales process.

- Train and upskill your staff so they become more effective, improve their performance and increase their sales.

- Design campaigns for existing customers and increase retention by upselling, cross-selling, asking for referrals and expanding their relationship with you.

- Assign responsibility and accountability for marketing projects. A large share of your marketing budget should be spent on marketing analytics so that you are able to measure the performance, results and ROI.

These are just some of the ways you can get better results without additional costs or efforts. Every time you review and analyse your data, you can tweak and improve your campaigns to generate higher returns for those and future campaigns.

RUNNING THE SAME EVENTS AGAIN

Running nine competitions over four years in my second restaurant provided a good learning curve and opportunity to improve this strategy. The first competition only ran for five weeks and, for the effort that was required, this was too short. The next competition ran for four weeks, and the same was true. The third and fourth competitions ran for nine and twelve weeks and provided much better results. Running the same strategy with incremental tweaks and improvements led to better results each time.

The eighty/twenty rule

The Pareto principle, also known as the eighty/twenty rule, helps you plan and experiment with your marketing mix. The Pareto principle states that roughly 80% of consequences come from 20%

of causes. Management consultant Joseph M Juran developed the concept in the context of quality control and improvement,[30] naming it after Italian economist Vilfredo Pareto who, while at university in 1896, noticed that 80% of the land in Italy was owned by 20% of the population.[31] Pareto carried out surveys in other countries and, to his surprise, found that a similar distribution of wealth applied. The Pareto principle has since been applied to many other industries and situations; that it adds up to 100 provides a nice symmetry and demonstrates the level of imbalance.

Applying this rule to everything in your marketing activities and opportunities allows you to stay committed to finding new and better ways to keep ahead of the game in your industry while maintaining a stable marketing mix. By spending 20% of your budget on experimenting, you can see what opportunities lead to growth and satisfactory revenue returns. Use the other 80% to pay for the marketing strategies you already know work.

Proven campaigns with a solid infrastructure in place can be repeated with minimal adjustments to maintain good performance and stability in revenue. New campaigns are demanding but the effort can be worth it, as you may find opportunities that make a big

---

30 Juran, 'The history of quality', Blog (4 March 2020), www.juran.com/blog/a-guide-to-the-pareto-principle-80-20-rule-pareto-analysis, accessed 9 September 2021
31 V Pareto, H Bousquet and G Busino, *Cours d'Économie* (Librairie Droz, 1964)

difference to your sales and profitability. When you learn something new from a campaign experiment, any 'gold nuggets' that are discovered can be scaled alongside what's working.

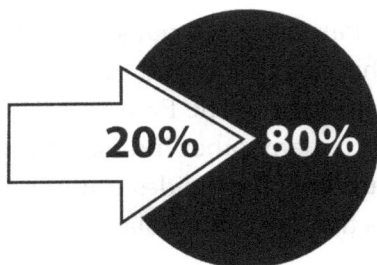

You can see various examples of Pareto's principle in action in marketing:

- 80% of profits come from 20% of customers

- 80% of sales come from 20% of products

- 80% of sales come from 20% of advertising

APPLYING THE EIGHTY/TWENTY RULE

With my marketing goals and objectives, not every strategy aimed to attract more sales. The marketing campaigns and competitions intended to drive sales made up 80% of my marketing mix, with 20% of my activities dedicated to increasing brand awareness through social media news posts, blogs, loyalty programmes, sponsorships and community programmes.

Innovation

Marketing is the bridge between your business and your customers. It is how you reach potential customers and deliver the value you have promised. It is not possible to stand still in today's world. To succeed, you need to adapt and continually apply an innovation strategy to your marketing plan and activities.

Innovation helps you achieve a better ROI. It is a form of quality management that focuses on making small incremental improvements to a process, rather than major changes. You can use this strategy to achieve goals such as increasing the accuracy of targeting, improving product or service quality, increasing customer satisfaction, or providing higher quality leads to your sales team.

You should be constantly developing and improving your marketing and striving for ways to perfect your activities to better serve your customers. In fast-developing markets, forward-thinking businesses have an edge over competitors. By testing and measuring your campaigns, you get a better understanding of what your customers want. This puts you in a stronger position to meet and exceed their expectations.

By evolving to be more connected with your customers, you add value to your business and reduce marketing spend wastage. Marketing budgets are valuable and every dollar spent should be used to better serve your customers. Wasted marketing budget on tactics that do not work could have been spent on improving your customers' experiences.

When prospective customers are making decisions about future purchases, they use the internet to gather preliminary information about products and companies. This means your website and Google My Business account are especially important, as your search engine ranking will determine whether your prospects find your business or your competitors' first. When comparing businesses, customers can easily detect those that do not innovate, as certain things will seem old or out of date. Look at your business and see if you are doing tasks in the most effective way or if there is somewhere you could innovate and make an impact more easily.

INNOVATIVE WAYS TO ATTRACT NEW CUSTOMERS

Finding new and different ways to market my restaurants was challenging. Keeping my regular campaigns active was good for customer retention, but I was trying to think of innovative ways to attract new customers.

One of my favourite staff activities was a name card draw. At one of our regular meetings, I had the staff write names on blank name tags and attach these to their uniforms. They came up with some clever names

– Superman, Princess, Drama Queen, Clown, Miss Perfect, Prankster, Captain, Sidekick etc, and they had fun coming up with the different personas. Every day, at the start of their shift, each staff member would pick a random name tag to wear for that day and take on that persona. This activity built camaraderie among the team, but the customers loved it too. It was fun to see a shy young dishwasher become Superman. I noticed that it began to attract a new range of customers who were curious to see what it was about, which was the purpose of this innovative activity.

Summary

In this chapter, we learned how analysis of your marketing results and reports, as well as the wider environment of your business, helps you to improve current strategies to attract more customers to spend more money through innovative ideas and activities.

As a marketer you need to stay aware of and up to date with trends and changes in the market, and continue to innovate. You can do this by gathering analytics across your marketing channels, campaigns and activities to generate insights into how your marketing programmes are performing. These insights will enable you to improve your marketing efforts and increase your revenue and profitability. Post-campaign analysis enables you to reflect on a specific campaign, its successes and what could have been done differently. This will help you to improve future campaigns and your business going forward. Some ways to improve your campaigns might be to run them for longer or repeatedly, increasing the number of campaigns you run, training staff and designing new, innovative campaigns to attract both existing and new customers.

We learned that applying the Pareto principle, also known as the eighty/twenty rule, is a good way to plan and experiment with your marketing mix by spending 20% of your marketing budget on experimenting with your marketing strategies and 80% on what is already proven to work. Applying this principle, you can use innovation alongside tried and tested methods to develop a marketing plan and strategies that are adaptable and unique to your business and customers' needs.

14

Optimising

With marketing optimisation, you use the data and metrics you have collected with the specific purpose of informing your future marketing decisions and increasing your ROI. As a business owner, you will want to spend your marketing budget as efficiently and intelligently as possible. In other words, you want to spend your money on the campaigns and methods that work. This will give you the best ROI.[32] The optimisation process involves taking a good look at your marketing campaign data and reports and deciding which campaigns you should keep running, which you should pause, which you could do differently and which you should cancel altogether.

---

32 H Friedman, 'The complete guide to marketing optimization', Improvado (23 September 2019), https://improvado.io/blog/marketing-optimization-guide accessed 20 May 2021

The thing about marketing is that you are never 100% certain that what you are doing is getting the best results. Running tests to see which elements of the marketing strategy are generating the highest returns is a good way to find the right balance between methods and justify marketing spend. When you find something that is working and bringing customers in, you can optimise it further by making tweaks to see if you can increase conversion rates even more. By being clear about what you want a campaign to achieve, you can measure the results and make optimal decisions going forward.

Optimisation is an ongoing regular practice; by having a process and system, you get insights on how to keep improving your marketing strategy and individual campaigns, maintain overall performance and meet the KPIs for the business.

FINDING THE BEST OFFER

I ran a quarterly promotion in a kids' club newsletter via the shopping centre where my second restaurant was located. I changed the offer over the years. I initially started with a free milkshake but then changed the free item to a babyccino, mini Dutch pancakes, a muffin, a scone and other combinations. Each campaign was measured for ROI. By having many offers using this one channel, it was much easier to optimise this campaign. They were all successful, but by comparing the ROI, average spend and overall sales for each offer, I saw that the offers of a free milkshake

and mini Dutch pancakes returned the best overall
results.

Attribution

The path to getting customers is becoming more
complex, with an average of six to eight touches across
multiple channels and devices before a customer makes
a purchase.[33] It is important to get a clear view of which
channels contribute to your customer conversion. Attribution tells you which touchpoints, marketing channels, campaigns and interactions led to conversions
and which did not. You can find out which channels
are converting and why and what steps can be taken to
boost those channels that aren't doing so well.

When you know what influences your customers
and to what extent, you can optimise your marketing
toward conversions. Attribution data can be used to
plan future campaigns and measure the performance
of previous campaigns specifically in terms of which
were the most cost-effective and influential, using
digital metrics.

It is difficult to track the entire journey of a customer,
as they may use multiple devices, browsers and
platforms, though you can be certain of their

---

33 L Beasley, 'Why it takes 7 to 13+ touches to deliver a qualified sales
    lead (Part 1)', *Online Marketing Institute* (10 October 2013), https://
    tinyurl.com/8umnxbk2, accessed 9 September 2021

last interaction prior to converting or making a purchase. Evaluating the touchpoints of a customer's journey along their pathway to buying from you is an essential part of cross-channel marketing – you need to know what caused your customer to act. By using attribution data, you will get a better understanding of which activities drive the most results for marketing strategies.

MULTI-TOUCH ATTRIBUTION

In my second restaurant, I ran competitions three times per year. The purpose of the competitions was to collect a database, increase sales, forge a new business partnership and reward customers. These competitions attracted over 1,400 entries and a clean database of several hundred new email addresses. (My regular customers would have multiple entries, which is why I used the two metrics: entries and new email addresses).

These email addresses would be added to the database that I sent regular monthly newsletters to with special offers and latest news. Many of these recipients would come into the restaurant regularly and would use a loyalty card that gave them their tenth coffee for free. They were also encouraged to 'like' my Facebook page.

This was a multi-touch attribution model for my marketing: competition, email newsletter, loyalty card, Facebook page.

From engaging with one competition, a customer would have multiple touchpoints in the lifetime of their patronage.

Split testing

Split, or A/B testing, involves conducting multiple types of experiments with the goal of improving the results of a marketing campaign. Split testing allows you to compare two different versions of a campaign – the original and a variation – to see which performs better. There should only be one difference between the two so that the reason behind any variation in performance is clear.

One way to split test a marketing campaign is to test different colours on your CTA button to see which has the biggest impact on clicks and, therefore, on overall results. This type of testing is valuable because, when you create your campaigns, it can be tempting to rely on intuition to predict what will make people click and convert. Basing marketing decisions off a 'feeling' can be detrimental, it is better to do a split test. Some common mistakes that happen when you are not methodical in your testing procedures include:

1. Testing without a reason – tests should identify what is not converting

2. Following other people's recommendations – what works for someone else may not work for you, use your own data

3. Not following best practice – make sure you have all the right elements and design

4. Testing things that will not make a difference – focus on changes that have a big impact on your results

5. Assuming that split testing will make a difference – it is still only one part of the conversion equation[34]

Split testing originated with direct mail and print advertising campaigns, which were tracked using different phone numbers for each version of the campaign to see which generated the most calls. Today you can split test any type of marketing campaign, including banner and text ads, email subject lines and many other options. Testing also helps reveal ROI for a set of campaigns across different platforms; this can be measured easily when tests are created with quantifiable goals attached to them.

WHICH OFFER IS BEST?

When you have multiple campaigns going at the same time, you can test which offer is generating the best results. One of my favourite formulas was the email newsletter promotion (no cost), where there was a free item on offer, either free mini-Dutch pancakes or a free coffee. It was interesting to review the redemption results each month and see which was the most popular item and the average sale amount. In one month,

---

34 T Vrountas, 'What is split testing? 8 steps to follow for your next campaign', Instapage (9 February 2020), https://instapage.com/blog/what-is-split-testing, accessed 20 May 2021

for example, free coffees produced sales of $14.95 over eighteen customers and the free mini pancakes produced sales of $11.76 over twenty-one customers. From testing these campaigns regularly, I could see that free coffees would result in a higher average spend but attract fewer customers. I could use this information to create other opportunities to attract more customers or increase their spend, and use either of these popular free items as the call-to-action.

Repetition

The more people see or hear something, the more they remember it. The most successful brands tend to have the most recognisable messages. Repetition is key to recognition; it's how consumers learn that a brand is in the marketplace and forms a 'top of mind awareness'. Through frequent messaging, you can ensure people remember your business. Familiarity with a brand develops a level of trust. The more familiar people are with a brand and the more they trust it, the more likely they are to purchase from that business. From Coca-Cola to McDonalds, the most frequently seen and heard brands become more successful. This should influence your marketing activities; the more messaging and activities you are involved with, the more likely people are to recognise your brand's presence, increasing trust and sales. Remember: prolific beats perfect.

Using multiple channels – for example, social media, video and online advertising – to share the same message makes it easier to include repetition in your marketing strategy. This is what we refer to as a marketing mix.

A WINNING FORMULA

For every promotion in my second restaurant, the offers were the same, 'buy one, get one free'. It was my most successful offer that always attracted customers and I used it in different campaigns across different channels. The staff could redeem the voucher easily, as no training was required to update them with any changes, and customers knew that we ran this offer regularly and would be on the lookout for it. When you have a good formula, repeating it creates a winning strategy.

Emulating

Emulating is copying, duplicating or improving something that someone else has done to make it work for you. You can emulate your competition, a successful concept or a strategy you have seen get results in a different industry. Check out what your competitors are doing to get ideas. What works for one hairdressing salon will likely work equally well for another hairdressing salon in a similar or even different location. When you look at what your competitors are doing, you will get some idea of what is working and what is not. Borrow successful competitors' strategies and create your own versions aligned with your brand

and business. Never duplicate content word for word and do not reproduce images without written permission and giving due credit. Simply do what they did and make it your own. If the content worked for them, it could work for you.

Emulation is vital if you want your business to succeed. Emulate what you can see working and is likely to give you results. If you can emulate a successful marketing campaign, this will avoid wasting money trying to come up with new ideas. The best way to do this efficiently is to set up a simple system using a template. When you see something that is working right, copy everything about it into a template and try it out; if it works, try it across different platforms to see if they work equally successfully. Ideally, you will take the idea and improve on it, for example making it more customer friendly. Improving on what already exists is a great way to get your business seen and is one of the smartest marketing moves you can make.

COPYING AND IMPROVING

When you know what other businesses are doing, you can use the same strategy, or improve on it and make it better. I did this with my kids' promotions. I saw what other hospitality providers were offering, tested the same offers, saw what got results and came up with my own versions that worked fantastically for us.

AI

Using AI technology, you can track a customer and learn their behaviours to improve the interaction between your customers and your business. AI platforms use intelligent, machine-learning systems that can help you allocate marketing budget and improve your ROI, by identifying trends and common occurrences and predicting common insights, responses and reactions. This enables you to understand the root causes of customer behaviour and the likelihood of certain actions repeating.

Using AI, you can take data and targeting to a whole new level – the analytics it uses can go as deep as understanding people on an individual basis. You can use this to identify potential clients or buyers and deliver the content that is most relevant to them. You can use AI-enabled dashboards to gain a comprehensive view of the campaign elements that work, spot patterns, replicate and adjust campaigns to see increased success. AI tools drive smart campaign analytics and enhanced reporting insights; they are much faster than humans, freeing up your time to focus on strategy.

Some examples of popular AI marketing methods are:

- **Recommendations for products:** Companies use AI to predict customer behaviour on their sites, including the likelihood of a future purchase.

Example: when searching for a Monopoly boardgame, when you scroll down the webpage other similar games will be suggested based on your search for Monopoly.

- **AI enhanced advertising:** Google and Facebook use algorithms based on machine learning to provide searchers with advertising that matches the interests and channels that a person uses. Remarketing is a typical example of this. Example: if you are interested in yoga, you will be shown ads for yoga products in your newsfeed, banner ads, and inside other websites that you look at.

- **Predictive analytics:** Companies use AI to enhance the customer service experience by looking at data and predicting trends. This information is used to make decisions for the future. Example: Amazon will boost their sales by forecasting possible future purchases for each customer based on what that person has bought in the past.

AI REMARKETING

I went to Cairns for a holiday. Beforehand, I researched flights, accommodation and things to do while there. When I started this research, I began receiving emails about Cairns; my Facebook feed featured information about what was coming up in Cairns; I got notifications from coupon sites with special offers for this destination. All these companies were using remarketing methods, a form of AI. It is present everywhere and you can sometimes feel like the internet is stalking you. It is advertisers using data captured from your digital footprint to keep reminding you that they have what you are looking for.

Summary

In this chapter, we looked at how optimisation of marketing activities and strategies is an ongoing practice that you need to be continually engaged in. Optimisation is a process and requires a system, which can include attribution, split testing, repetition, emulation and use of AI.

Marketing attribution reveals the touchpoints of a customer's journey. Your aim is to find the last attribution point before a purchase so that you can understand what caused the customer to make that purchase. Split testing, or A/B testing, is a way to test and improve your campaign by trying slightly different versions of it. This enables you to make decisions based on data rather than gut feeling. When you've found what works, repetition is key. Successful brands usually have established and repeated messages, slogans and recognisable logos. Familiarity breeds trust, so keep repeating your message to attract more customers.

One way to keep innovating is to emulate. This means looking at competitors in your industry and seeing what works for them, then taking those ideas and adapting them for your business with your branding. Ideally, you will tweak and improve upon your competitors' ideas, so they work even better for you.

At the forefront of innovation is AI, using which you can track your customers' behaviour and learn more about what they want. This enables you to remarket to them based on what you know they are interested in.

All these tools and methods will help you to more finely target customers and attract them to your business.

15
Forecasting

F orecasting is a technique that is used to determine what you will do in the future with your marketing. It involves making a prediction of what the future might look like so that you are able to set achievable, relevant goals and create plans – a bit like using a crystal ball to predict and plan for your business' future performance. But a crystal ball is just a ball, the future is not here yet, and the best laid plans don't have certainty. Decisions made today will affect future outcomes. The need for forecasting in this environment is significant, as your positioning can be affected by the constant changes in technology, the social and political landscape and globalisation. It is vital for your business that you try to anticipate change as accurately as possible so that your business can not only survive but thrive, by gaining a competitive advantage.[35]

In this chapter, we will look at the different forecasting techniques and methods you can use when creating your marketing plan and marketing mix. Gathering and analysing marketing metrics will again help you to make informed marketing decisions for the future and to review performance through quantitative and qualitative assessment of marketing campaigns. This will help ensure you are directing future marketing budget to the right areas.

Creating and implementing a marketing strategy affects the whole business, so accuracy is important in forecasting. If a change or trend is overestimated, you will waste time, money and effort. If it is underestimated, you might be faced by a sudden, unexpected level of demand that your business is not ready to meet, potential sales can be lost and your reputation damaged. Forecasting is, ultimately, guesswork, but basing this on historical data makes it as informed and accurate as possible.

Having a process to follow makes forecasting easier and more successful. The basic steps of a forecasting process are to:

- Determine the purpose

---

35 Forecasting Page, 'The purpose and need for forecasting' (no date), https://sites.google.com/site/forecastingprojectvatech/home/how-forecasting-works-implementation, accessed 20 May 2021

- Establish the time frame

- Select a technique

- Gather and analyse data

- Make the forecast

- Monitor the forecast[36]

USING YOUR CRYSTAL BALL

In business, you use forecasting in many areas of operations. Rosters are made in advance, as are stock supply orders. Marketing itself is a form of forecasting, aiming to attract future customers to the business. In my restaurants, I would use historical data and my experience to try and predict the future. When things did not work out as I had hoped or expected, I would often say 'my crystal ball was cloudy that day.'

Historical data

Look to the past to determine the future. Using historical data is one of the best and simplest ways to forecast accurately.[37] Historical data is the data that

---

36 Forecasting Page, 'The purpose and need for forecasting' (no date), https://sites.google.com/site/forecastingprojectvatech/home/how-forecasting-works-implementation, accessed 20 May 2021

37 M Newlands, 'How to use historic data to predict marketing campaign outcomes', Econsultancy (9 June 2015), https://econsultancy.com/how-to-use-historic-data-to-predict-marketing-campaign-outcomes, accessed 20 May 2021

you have collected from and about past campaigns and the metrics for these activities. It can be generated either manually or automatically and be used to gain insight into how past customer behaviour relates to the future. Through detailed examination of historical marketing strategies and campaign behaviour, metrics and results you will have a longer-term perspective that may prove useful in developing a viable marketing strategy for the future, improving on existing activities, performance tracking and planning for major events or seasonality. Historical data is an important input when strategising and creating future campaigns. The more campaign history you can draw from, the more insights you can uncover – and the more mistakes you can avoid repeating. Remember though to keep historical data in context and consider whether it is relevant in the present marketing conditions. Capturing as much data and information as possible is useful for making decisions in the future and gives you more freedom to experiment with your campaigns.

By using historical data to predict the outcomes of your future efforts, you will avoid wasting time and money on campaigns that do not work. Everything you do will be much more effective, improving your ROI on each campaign. With so many other businesses using data analytics in their marketing activities, you need to also be making use of these methods to ensure you remain competitive.

HISTORICAL DATA-DRIVEN STRATEGIES

In my restaurants, I always based my forecasting on historical data. I knew exactly when the busiest day of the year would be and when the quieter months were. I find that the first two years in business are the hardest, as you are flying blind and experimenting with anything and everything in the hope that something will work. It was only when I had collected a lot of data over time that I could identify and improve on the strategies that worked, drop those that didn't and experiment with new channels. By the time I got to my third restaurant, I had great strategies that had worked for me previously, I only needed to test whether they would be as successful in the new venue. Historical data enabled me to fast-track my previous business' marketing activities.

Qualitative forecasting

Sometimes, historical data is not available or relevant. In this case, qualitative techniques can be used to bring together and consider various factors in a logical, unbiased and systematic way. This type of forecasting is usually applied to intermediate or long-term decisions and is based on more subjective information that cannot be easily measured. Qualitative forecasting can predict changes in sales patterns and customer behaviour based on the experience and judgement of senior staff and outside experts.

Methods of qualitative forecasting include:

- **The Delphi method:** This method uses multiple questionnaires completed by a panel of industry experts or specialists to gather their opinions regarding the business or product. The goal is to reach a group consensus of executive opinions and base your forecasting on the results.

- **In-house expertise:** The staff members with the most expertise use their in-depth knowledge to make predictions. This method can be implemented easily and quickly without the need for elaborate statistics.

- **Market research:** This is the process of testing the popularity of a product or service by gauging the reactions of prospective customers. Market research allows businesses to identify their target markets and seek ideas and responses from customers to fine-tune their products.

Qualitative methods are most beneficial for newer or smaller companies who lack historical and/or quantitative data to base forecasts on. Even for established businesses, the information gained from qualitative forecasting methods can provide additional insight from industry experts that objective and/or numerical data cannot produce. Qualitative analysis relates to perceptions of branding, trustworthiness and customer satisfaction. AI is currently unable to perform this kind of analysis, so reviewing these perspectives provides a valuable contribution to creating a more positive and holistic experience for the customer.

QUALITATIVE FORECASTING WHEN STARTING A BUSINESS

When starting a new restaurant or business, I used qualitative forecasting for marketing. Drawing on my own expertise and that of others in my industry, plus lots of research, I made the best, most informed decisions I could for the business. I wouldn't know for sure which campaigns would be successful, or if I could find customers using a particular channel, but I used what I had available to move forward. Once I had done something, I could begin to collect data that I could use in the future.

Quantitative forecasting

When planning the future, look to your past.[38] Quantitative forecasting relies on data that can be measured and manipulated, and is a hugely valuable forecasting method for established businesses that have been collecting objective historical data over months or years. Quantitative forecasting uses this data to predict future sales, revenue and expenses. Statistical data from past campaigns and strategies is used

---

38 N Marcotullio, 'The top 5 methods for quantitative sales forecasting', Map My Customers (2020), https://mapmycustomers.me/blog/the-top-3-methods-for-quantitative-sales-forecasting, accessed 20 May 2021

to evaluate what is happening right now and what direction the numbers are trending in to give the most accurate predictions of what may occur in the future. This method is best for making short-term forecasts, as past trends are more like to reoccur sooner than in the long term. It also allows you to get a general idea of where your business is headed.

Types of quantitative forecasting include:

- **Time series analysis:** This uses data from a specific strategy or campaign to get a clear sense of patterns over time, indicating that these will continue into the future. This type of analysis can identify cyclical patterns, trends, growth rates and any irregularity or variation in the data.

- **Causal methods:** These methods consider unplanned or unintended factors (like weather or a major competitor with a similar offering) that affect your marketing. This is a more advanced technique that can 'look' further into the future than time series analysis, as it also incorporates market research.

Quantitative forecasting exposes patterns and identifies trends over a specific length of time. Using this type of forecasting, you can predict what marketing activities are best to use now and what to plan for the future, with clear data to support these decisions and provide input for formulas that will help drive future.

USING YOUR OWN HISTORICAL DATA

I collected five years' worth of sales and marketing data from my second restaurant, to check or estimate my performance regularly. I used it for forecasting with rostering, ordering, and marketing campaigns. This was the best data to have because it was my own and was relevant to what I did and what I was doing, and I could keep using it in the future.

Customer desires

Are you curious about what it is that brings people to your business and encourages them to buy products or services from you? Once a upon a time, shoppers relied on a salesperson with excellent skills to help them find what they wanted. Today's customers have limitless options, especially with social media. Advances in marketing technology, data collection and analytics make it possible to deliver a new form of the personal service provided to yesteryear's sales staff. Using detailed customer data, a business can create highly customised offers that get the attention of customers with the right offer at the right time, at the right price and via the right channel. Only a few businesses can do this well. You need to be constantly learning from your customers and adapting your strategies based on that learning. Monitoring your online conversations and social media sites for customer research purposes will give you insight and knowledge of what is being said about your business. Analytics will tell which devices your customers use, how they navigate around your site and what products/services they are searching for – this gives you important insights into their interests, needs and habits. With detailed knowledge of who your customers are and what they like, you can identify your ideal customer or niche and target your campaigns toward these people.

Knowing and learning from your customers is crucial to the success of your business. Once you have this knowledge, you can use it to persuade and influence potential and existing customers by tailoring your marketing messages to fulfil their desires. You also need to remember that marketing evolves and changes, so it is important to continue learning to keep up with your existing customers and attract new ones.

LISTEN TO CUSTOMER SUGGESTIONS

In all my restaurants, I used my specials board to try out customer menu suggestions. I would test a customer request out as a special to see if it was a winner. If these dishes sold well, I would add them to the menu. I only updated my main menu once a year, to increase prices and drop/add new items, so it was important that I got these decisions right.

Winning formulas

Sadly, you cannot find winning formulas on Google and 'copy and paste' them to your business or in your marketing activities. You will develop these for your own business based on activities you have done in the past that you know always work, the activities that provide the best results, have great ROI, are efficient and effective. When you have a winning formula, it can be implemented with very little effort and you win (and profit) every single time.

Sometimes the formula takes a while to create, and there are many factors and characteristics that contribute to it. It takes time, experimentation, diligence and determination to find out what is guaranteed to drive results for your business. Think of it like a puzzle: there are many pieces and components, and a missing piece will compromise the whole picture. Integrity is an important element to the formula, as is a focus on both the future and the present.

The insights you will have gained from your marketing and campaign reports regarding the tactics that worked and those that didn't are essential inputs to your winning formula. You want your formula to increase cashflow into the business, so focus on the following things:

- **ROI per campaign:** This is how many sales were generated minus the cost of the campaign.

- **Sales revenue:** This is how much income was generated from a single campaign.

- **Cost per campaign:** This is how much money you spent on creating and promoting each campaign (this needs to include wage costs related to producing content).

- **Number of customers:** This is how many people came and spent money in your business because of a particular campaign.

- **Average sale per customer:** This gives you a value per customer, which allows you to compare different campaigns on different channels.

You can use software to give you these values; you do not need to be great at maths or making complex Excel spreadsheets to create your winning formula.

FINDING YOUR WINNING FORMULA

The winning formula for marketing in my second restaurant took a few years to create and many iterations of the strategies I had implemented over this time. The first component was an action plan and adding the dates into my schedule to make sure that activities would happen. Secondly, a style guide, the offer or CTA of 'buy one get one free', advertising mix of three paid sources, promotional mix (competitions, email marketing, newsletters and social media posts) and community programs took time to perfect and refine. Lastly, collecting the sales linked to a campaign gave me the knowledge to make decisions about forecasting future activities and operations in the business. All these items when constructed became my winning formula to run the marketing for this restaurant.

Decision-making

As a business owner, you make important decisions on behalf of your business every day, small decisions and big ones. How much money should you spend on marketing? What CTA should you use? There is a whole range of factors that influence your marketing decisions; having a clear understanding of what these are will improve the quality of the outcomes in your marketing.

As a marketing manager or business owner, you need to look at what contributes to a successful outcome; it can be the marketing mix, customer behaviour, competitors, or the economy. Decisions are made by evaluating your forecasts, reporting, personal knowledge of the situation, evidence and alternatives.

IF YOU OWN YOUR BUSINESS, YOU MAKE DECISIONS

As a business owner, you are always the one that needs to make the big decisions. How much money would you spend on marketing? What CTA should you use? Every item requires a decision, and since you are the business owner, it comes down to you.

For bigger and more complex decisions, you may need to use a combination of reasoning, facts, management and intuition (your 'gut feeling'). You still need to pay attention to what is needed to get a successful outcome, don't just go with your gut instinct or judgement, as this may not lead to the best decision in a particular situation. Using a decision-making process alongside your data, reports and forecasts will help you to make the best, most well-rounded and considered judgements to continually move your business forward.

There are seven steps in the decision-making process:

1. Identify the decision

2. Gather the relevant information

3. Identify the alternatives

4. Weigh the evidence

5. Choose among the alternatives

6. Take action

7. Review your decision[39]

Understanding the decision-making process is key if you want to solve a problem and get great outcomes. As a business owner, you will need to make strategic and tactical decisions about potential opportunities,

---

39 University of Massachusetts, 'Decision-making process' (23 September 2016), www.umassd.edu/fycm/decision-making/process, accessed 30 June 2021

planning, implementation, performance and control every day as a key requirement of your marketing management skillset.

Summary

In this chapter, we looked at how forecasting can help to determine what the future holds for your business and industry. Good forecasting is mainly based on historical data, adding in any new knowledge and market information to the process.

Forecasting can be both, or either, qualitative or quantitative. Qualitative forecasting is subjective and relies on data that cannot measured. You should use these techniques when you don't have much data available, for example when you are just starting out or trying something for the first time.

Quantitative forecasting must be objective and based on data that can be measured. One of the best ways to determine what will happen in the future is to look at the past. Historical data can predict the outcomes of your future efforts, helping you to avoid wasting time and money on campaigns that will not work and focus on the activities that you know will continue to provide the best results with minimum effort.

All forecasting relates to and depends on your customers' behaviour and desires, so knowing and learning from your customers is imperative for your marketing, now and into the future. You should continue to learn from them and adapt your strategies based on what you discover about their behaviour and preferences, tailoring your message to attract them to your business.

When you implement a strategy of forecasting based on historical data, expert/market knowledge and customer desires, you can create a winning formula and win every single time. Sometimes the process takes a while to create, and there are many factors that will contribute towards your formula for success.

As a business owner, you need to make decisions about potential opportunities and implementing marketing campaigns. You are making decisions every day, both big and small, and every decision affects the success of your business. A decision-making process will ensure you take all the relevant factors into consideration and never rely too heavily on one decision driver.

Conclusion

M arketing spreads the word about your business and encourages potential customers to spend their money with you. Every business needs to do it. Without it, you cannot connect with your people and let them know the opportunities your business provides for them.

Researching and understanding every aspect of your business, including your customers, gives you the ability to make sound business decisions. When you assess your business' strengths and weaknesses, you can see how your customers view your products and services.

Understanding which marketing strategies and campaigns will be most effective is the first step to a great marketing plan. By taking steps to understand your customers better, you will ensure that your marketing efforts are relevant, targeted and personalised. This allows you to build and maintain relationships with your customers and implement ongoing strategies to ensure your business will flourish and improve its bottom line.

A key objective within your marketing should be to identify new opportunities and determine where current ones can be optimised and improved. To succeed, you need to have a balanced mix of marketing activities and understand the value of each activity and platform, attracting customers via different channels and strategies.

Streamlining your marketing can be an easy process if you are already active in this area. If you are not, just get started. Once you are engaged in a marketing activity, you can track and measure your results. You can then test and improve on these activities to get the best outcomes for your business. By focusing on the five areas of the methodology presented in this book, you will be able to create a personalised system for your business and boost your results.

You want to make it easy for you, as the business owner, to know where to focus your efforts and budget. This book shows you which areas you need integrate into your marketing operations in order to create a marketing system that will work for your business. A personalised marketing system that is aligned to your business guarantees results. It is easy to replicate and improve. The simpler the system, the easier it is to implement and for your staff to follow it. A system guarantees accuracy and good results, which will be evident when you generate reports for review, analysis, and to make decisions to improve the performance of the business.

If you want to live a lifestyle that you love, building a profitable business with a great ROI is the first step to fulfilling all of your wants and desires. Success means looking at the right data and using it to grow your business.

Resources

Part One – Initiate

Australian Taxation Office benchmarking – www.ato.gov.au/Business/Small-business-benchmarks

Canva – www.canva.com

DISC – www.discprofile.com/what-is-disc

Fivrr – www.fiverr.com

Google My Business – www.google.com/intl/en_au/business

Hootsuite – www.hootsuite.com

Marketing plan – https://business.gov.au/planning/business-plans/how-to-write-your-marketing-plan

Pexels – www.pexels.com

Pixabay – https://pixabay.com

Sendible – www.sendible.com

Unsplash – https://unsplash.com

Upwork – www.upwork.com

Part Two – Ideas

Active Campaign – www.activecampaign.com

Amazon's Associate Programme – https://affiliate-program.amazon.com

Mailchimp – https://mailchimp.com

PLR products – www.theplrstore.com

Trello – https://trello.com

Part Three – Implement

Answer the Public – https://answerthepublic.com

Google Trends – https://trends.google.com/trends

Part Four – Identify

Google Forms – www.google.com.au/forms/about

Maralytics – https://maralytics.com

Survey Monkey – www.surveymonkey.com

Part Five – Innovate

Google Analytics – https://analytics.google.com/analytics/web

Templates and resources mentioned in this book

I have created a Google Drive folder to provide templates and resources mentioned in this book. Use this link to access it: https://bit.ly/3ansfnc

Acknowledgements

Thank you to my son, Lachlan, for always listening to me when I needed to verbalise and get ideas clear while writing some of the sections of this book. Thank you also to the rest of my family and friends for supporting me through the writing process.

Special thanks go to Lucy McCarraher, Joe Gregory, Helen Lanz, Susan Furber and Abi Angus from Rethink Press, Suzon Bishwas for the graphics, and to Mike Clark and the team at Dent for the fantastic Key Person of Influence business accelerator programme and the book challenge. Without them, this book would not have been written and published.

Thank you to my beta readers, Alison, Jennie, Glashie, Kate, Evie, Tarn and Angie for helping me to make the manuscript more reader friendly.

The Author

Miriam van Heusden is the founder and CEO of Maralytics. She is a restaurateur, business coach, certified professional vocational trainer, food and travel consultant, and outdoor adventure lover. A mother and business owner herself, she knows first-hand the importance of creating a healthy balance between work and family.

Miriam has owned three restaurants and is a highly regarded qualified trainer in the domestic and international education industry. She delivers diploma qualifications in hospitality, marketing, business, project and leadership management, and her industry experience and expertise in these areas are invaluable. She also provides training and development for all aspects of digital marketing.

Miriam's journey to creating Maralytics started when she was a restaurant owner and found herself frustrated at not being able to find a solution for her marketing activities. She wanted to analyse the results of her activities to see their effectiveness, easily make decisions and stop wasting money on marketing that did not work. From day one in the restaurant, she planned, negotiated, tracked and reported on all advertising and marketing campaigns. She knew from the start that analytics in business and marketing were important. Her philosophy is that numbers tell a story and the only way to improve performance is to avoid making the same mistakes twice.

Miriam looks at growth and structure as the core areas of business. She has created the Maralytics technology to dramatically grow sales and improve performance results through structured analysis. She is passionate about empowering business owners with the tools, skills and information to achieve better results and make easier decisions for success.

⊕ https://maralytics.com

⊕ https://about.me/miriam.van.heusden

in www.linkedin.com/in/miriam-van-heusden

www.ingramcontent.com/pod-product-compliance
Lightning Source LLC
Chambersburg PA
CBHW061157240326
R18026500001B/R180265PG41519CBX00020B/33